P9-BIQ-148

3 3

ECHO
of the
SOUL

ECHO
of the
SOUL

BT
741.3
N49
2000

The Sacredness of the Human Body

J. PHILIP NEWELL

SOUTHWESTERN
COLLEGE
Library
CHULA VISTA
CALIFORNIA

MOREHOUSE PUBLISHING

Copyright © 2000 J. Philip Newell

Morehouse Publishing
P.O. Box 1321
Harrisburg, PA 17105

Morehouse Publishing is a division of The Morehouse Group.

First published in 2000 by Canterbury Press Norwich (a publishing
imprint of Hymns Ancient & Modern Limited, a registered charity),
St. Mary's Works, St. Mary's Plain, Norwich, Norfolk NR3 3BH, U.K.

All rights reserved. No part of this book may be reproduced or
transmitted in any form or by any means, electronic or mechanical,
including photocopying, recording, or by any information storage
and retrieval system, without written permission from the publisher.

The Author asserts the moral right to be identified a the Author of
this work.

Cover design by Laurie Westhafer.

Cover photograph taken at Washington National Cathedral, Washington,
D.C., by William K. Geiger.

A catalog record for this book is available from the Library of Congress.
ISBN 0-1892-1874-X

Printed in the United States
01 02 03 04 05   10 9 8 7 6 5 4 3 2 1

To my eldest daughter
Rowan Elisabeth Mary
and the goodness of the human body

Contents

ACKNOWLEDGEMENTS

Bible quotations are from New Revised Standard Version (NRSV) 1989.

The publisher acknowledges with thanks permission to reproduce extracts from the following publications:

Edwin Muir, *An Autobiography*, by permission of Ethel Elizabeth Ross, © Chatto & Windus, 1980.

Edwin Muir, *Collected Poems*, © Faber and Faber, 1984.

PREFACE

Which one of us is not fascinated by the human body, by its mystery and its sensuousness, even if that fascination sometimes takes the form of confusion and doubt? We are rooted in our bodies. At birth, in our play and work together, in our love-making and at our death, it is not simply that we *have* bodies. It is more that we *are* bodies. And yet it is perplexing how little positive attention has been given to the body in the religious thought of the Western world. The writing of this book has sharpened my sense of the sacredness of the human body, including my own. I hope it will do the same for you.

The book came to birth during my last year in England before returning to Edinburgh. It was delivered initially as a series of talks at St Thomas's Cathedral in Portsmouth during Pentecost 1999. A group of twenty-five women and men met each week for seven weeks to meditate with me on the major themes of the book. I am extremely grateful to them for their willingness to share, and for the depth of perspective that emerged out of the silence of our meditations. It was also very good to be able to treat our bodies to a drink together afterwards at the pub opposite the Cathedral.

As always, the person to whom I am most indebted is Alison. When she married me over twenty years ago we took the traditional vow, 'With my body I honour you'. She has honoured me with her spirit and mind as well. This book has been shaped by all of these honourings.

J. Philip Newell
St Giles Cathedral
August 2000

INTRODUCTION

The starting point for spirituality in both Jewish and Christian practice is the Genesis 1 description of humanity made in the 'image' and 'likeness' of God.[1] This is the foundation text of our scriptural inheritance. Everything else that is said about us in the Scriptures needs to be read in relation to this truth. The image of God has been woven into the fabric of our being.

A nineteenth-century teacher in the Celtic tradition used the analogy of royal garments woven through with gold. If the golden thread were to be ripped out of the clothing the whole garment would unravel. So it is with the image of God woven into the mystery of our being. If somehow it were to be extracted we would cease to exist. The image of God is not simply a characteristic of our humanity. It is the essence of our being. Sin has not removed it but rather distorted it.

The description of humanity 'made in the image of God' refers to our physicalness as well as our spiritualness. The two are not separated. In Jewish belief the body is the soul in its outward form. Similarly the English poet William Blake describes the body as 'a portion of the soul'.[2] It is an expression of our inner being. As the ninth-century Irish teacher John Scotus Eriugena says, the body is an 'echo' of the soul.[3] It is a passing expression, but it carries the sounds of the depths of our being. Just as 'the soul is the image of God,' he says, so 'the body is the image of the soul'.[4]

In the biblical tradition, the Garden of Eden is our place of deepest identity. It represents our genesis in God and the essential goodness of our origins. It is not a place from which we are separated in space and time. Rather, it is a dimension within us from which we have become divorced. The Genesis picture is not of the destruction of Eden, but of Adam and Eve living in a type of exile from the Garden. Our place of profoundest identity has not been destroyed. Rather, we have become fugitives from it.

Genesis celebrates the goodness of creation at its birth and the sacredness of humanity made in the image of God. It also speaks, however, of sin 'lurking at the door'.[5] The picture is of evil at the doorway of life ready to pounce on all that is born. Given what we now know through modern psychological and ecological understanding, and our knowledge of the way in which an unborn child is affected by the mother's state of health and by the wider environment, we might want to say that sin is lurking inside the door of the womb. Life is infected by wrong at its earliest stages of development.

Creation is forever being born. It is continually issuing forth from the mystery of God, from the realm of 'the unseen' into the world of 'the seen', as the Scriptures say.[6] The biblical picture is that life at its inception is good but that its goodness immediately is threatened. All things fall under 'the power of sin', as the New Testament says.[7] They are imprisoned or held down by what is wrong. The goodness that is within us and within all life becomes like occupied territory. This leads St Paul to reflect on the tension that we experience in ourselves between good and evil. 'I do not do the good I want,' he says, 'but the evil I do not want is what I do.'[8] His 'inmost self', as he calls it, desires the good, but his false self pursues what is sinful. Redemption is about being reconnected to our true self.

Our Western Christian tradition often has given the impression, and at times explicitly has taught, that this tension is primarily between the soul and the body. The result has been a denigration of the human body and a distrust of our deepest physical energies. The biblical term 'the flesh', which refers to the sinful tendency in us to disregard our inmost self, incorrectly has been equated with 'the body'. 'The flesh' and 'the body' in the New Testament are different concepts. The consequences of the confusion have been disastrous. We have ended up obscuring the truth that our bodies are made in the image of God. When St Paul teaches that we are to live 'according to the spirit' rather than 'according to the flesh', he is not suggesting that we should not live according to the body.[9] It is precisely in our bodies that we are to live according to the spirit, rather than allowing ourselves, including our bodies, to be dictated to by what is opposed to our inmost being. The invitation is to be liberated, to be reconciled to what is deepest in us instead of being held in bondage to what is false in us.

The Irish novelist James Joyce describes one of his characters as living at a distance from himself. That is a fine description of how most of us live much of the time, at a distance from our true selves. Edwin Muir, the twentieth-century Scottish poet, in one of his poems speaks of the way in which 'evil and good' are bound inseparably together in the field of our lives and world, 'and nothing now can separate the corn and tares compactly grown'.[10] The imagery is of weeds choking the goodness of what has been planted originally in the depths of our being. 'Yet still from

Eden springs the root as clean as on the starting day',
writes Muir. The root is still there. It is our 'treasure trove',
he says, buried deep and needing to be rediscovered.
William Blake says that 'the Sanctuary of Eden' is still
within us but that the inner gate that leads to Eden is
'frozen' shut.[11] What is it that will open again that gateway
within us?

The Gospel of Christ, which means the good news of
Christ, is given to tell us not what we already know but
what we do not know. It is given not to tell us that we have
failed, because we already know that about ourselves. That
is not good news. It is given to tell us what we have forgotten, and that is who we are. Spirituality does not consist of
being told what to do. It consists of being reminded of who
we are. Only when we know who we are will we be clearer
about what we should do. The grace of repentance is about
turning around in our lives, but it is not about turning
around in order to become someone other than ourselves.
It is not about conforming to some exterior standard of
truth and good behaviour. Rather, it is about turning
around in order to be restored to what is deepest in us. It
is about becoming truly ourselves. The gift of grace
reawakens our memory of Eden. It begins to open again
within us the gateway to our true naturalness. As William
Blake says, grace bears us through darkness 'back safe' to
our humanity.[12] The problem is not our human nature.
The problem is our exile from true human nature. Grace
restores us again to ourselves.

The challenge is to discern the true self from the false
self, the authentic from the inauthentic. Repentance is not
simply about turning away from a false self out there. Evil
attaches itself like a cancer to what is good. The false self
lives off the true self. It grows on it. Part of repentance is to

discern the goodness in us that has become buried by evil. It is to identify deep in our mistakes and confusions the goodness that is a more authentic expression of our nature than our failings. It is to see sin as a misdirection of our truest energies. Repentance, therefore, is a painful operation. The false layers of who we are need to be severed from our true depths. As the twentieth-century Jewish teacher Abraham Kook says, 'this is the most inward kind of pain, through which a person is liberated from the dark servitude to his sins'.[13]

It is, of course, not always clear what is true in us and what is false. Where do we look for guidance in this journey of discernment? The intention of this book is to explore one of the 'sacred texts' of guidance, namely the human body. In my publication, *The Book of Creation*, I described how in the Celtic tradition there is a sense of the mystery of God being revealed through two 'texts'.[14] The first is Holy Scripture, referred to as the 'little' book. The second is Creation, known as the 'great' book. Just as we can be attentive to the living Word of God in the words of Scripture, so we can be alert to the expressions of God in the mystery of Creation. 'In the beginning was the Word', as St John says, and 'all things came into being through the Word'.[15] Our life and the whole life of creation have been uttered into being by God. It is, therefore, not away from life that we are to listen for intimations of the divine, but deep within all that has been created. The human body is a sacred text within the larger text of creation.

Celtic Christian spirituality has roots in the wisdom tradition of the Old Testament and especially in the mysticism of that tradition. Some of its main features bear a family likeness to later Jewish mysticism, which also was rooted in the Old Testament's wisdom tradition. Kabbalah, which means 'receiving', was a tradition of Jewish mysticism that emerged in medieval Europe. It taught a 'receiving' of ancient wisdom, both from the past and from deep within the human spirit. Kabbalistic tradition was attentive to Scripture, to creation and to the human body. These were like its three sacred texts. The human body was viewed as a microcosm of the sacred macrocosm of creation.

Throughout this book I shall be drawing on the great teachers of the Celtic tradition and the Jewish mystical tradition, as well as on others, like William Blake, who were influenced by the Kabbalah and its sense of the sacredness of the human body. Blake's emphasis on what he called 'the human form divine' is central to his way of seeing.[16] This is not to be naive about the brokenness of the human body and the human spirit. In Blake's artwork many of his human figures are crouched in a cave or in water, representing the shrunken or submerged state of humanity. Deeper still, however, is the splendour of the divine image waiting to be born again from within us.

Long before the Kabbalah there are signs of mystical experience in the Judaism of the Old Testament. The most significant figure in this tradition is the prophet Ezekiel in the sixth century BC. In his prophecy he includes what he calls 'visions of God'.[17] He sees a great cloud of brightness and at its centre 'something like gleaming amber'. It is what later mystics would call the cloud of 'unknowing', for always the self-disclosure of God is wrapped in mystery. Within the cloud is 'something like a throne', says Ezekiel, and above the throne 'something like a human form'. From the human form a brilliance of light and splendour issues forth. 'This', says Ezekiel, 'was the appearance of the likeness of the glory of the Lord.'[18]

Introduction

The Prophecy of Ezekiel's vision of God in human form prepares the way for later Jewish mystics to see the human body almost as an icon of divine light. It also prepares the way for Christian mystics to see Christ as the perfect embodiment of Light. In the kabbalistic tradition there developed a mystical understanding of what came to be known as the 'sefirot', derived from the word 'sapphire'. These were like jewels or shinings of the light of God in the human body. They were described as emanations of the brilliance of the divine image within us.

There are parallels between the Jewish understanding of 'sefirot' and the Eastern understanding of 'chakras', which are like centres of special energy in the human body. In the Jewish tradition the emanations of light are associated with the crown of the head, the centre of the forehead, the left and right arms, the heart, the genitals, the left and right legs, and the soles of the feet. These represent dimensions within us that have been neglected or forgotten and are needing to be recovered again. The major themes of this book are derived from this understanding of the human body.

The crown of the head represents the mystery of our being. What cannot be said about us is always greater than anything that can be said. The forehead is identified with the wisdom of the divine image within us, a way of seeing that is deeper than outward sight. The arms are associated with strength, the left arm with power and the right arm with love. Do we know the depth of strength that is within us, the strength for justice and the strength for love? The heart represents the beauty at the centre of our being, a beauty that is deeper than the ugliness of what we have done or become in our lives. The genitals are associated with creativity and our God-given capacity to bring into being what has never been before. The legs are identified with a glory and eternity that are like the pillars of life. If these were to be removed the temple of the universe itself would collapse. And the soles of our feet represent presence. What does it mean to be a person of presence, to be present to others and to ourself in love?

How willing are we to regard our bodies as sacred texts? For many religious people today the energy of the human body is feared because of its strong passions and confused urges. Others regard their physicalness with shame and distaste. There is a tendency, as we have noted, to divorce spirit from matter and to regard the sacred as higher than the body. As Edwin Muir says of the Scottish Calvinism of his day, 'The Word made flesh here is made word again.'[19] We are prone to turn the embodiment of God into an idea and look away from our bodies, rather than discovering that the sacred mystery is born in the matter of our bodies and relationships. On the other hand, in much of our secular culture, the body has become almost an object of worship, especially as it relates to the sexual. This idolising of the body, however, like the doubting of the body at the other end of the spectrum, also denies it a sacredness. In both extremes the body is demeaned.

The intention of this book is to reclaim the holy integration of the spiritual and the physical that is deep in our Jewish and Christian inheritance. Our bodies are sacred. They bear what Rabbi Heschel calls an 'ultimate preciousness'.[20]

I

THE MYSTERY OF THE SELF

In the tradition of the human body as sacred text the crown of the head is associated with mystery. It represents our undefinableness. What cannot be said about each one of us is always greater than anything that can be said. Science, psychology, spirituality provide us with tools to move further and further into the mystery of our being but never do they exhaust the soul's depths. Our own being is rooted in the fathomless mystery of God's being. Our truest identity is deeper than name and definition.

One woman, in meditating on this theme, found herself looking into a well. It was bottomless. She realised that she was looking into the well of her own being. As William Blake says, within us is a universe 'increasing inwards, into length and breadth, and height'.[1] It is of inexhaustible depth. If we begin to know the expansiveness of the mystery of our souls then we will begin to know the true nature of our beings, made in the image of the mystery of God. If we forget the unboundedness of who we are then we will live in a type of forgetfulness of our deepest origins. Deeper than anything that we can comprehend in ourselves is the mystery of our being. As the fourteenth-century Dominican mystic Meister Eckhart says, 'the soul is naked of all things that bear names'.[2] The core of our beings cannot be labelled.

Echo of the Soul

We are familiar with the crown of an infant's head at birth, and the way it is not yet hardened over in its bone structure. In its thin membrane covering there is a type of openness that is essential to the brain's expansion and growth. This part of a newborn's anatomy is known as the 'fontanelle', derived from the French for 'fountain'. The mystery of our lives is the fountain of our being for our own mystery streams forth from the mystery of God's being. As St Paul says, 'in God we live and move and have our being'.[3]

In the Prophecy of Ezekiel there is the vision of a cloud with a brightness of fire at its centre. At the heart of the cloud's brightness Ezekiel sees the likeness of a human form. 'This was the appearance of the likeness of the glory of the Lord,' says Ezekiel.[4] It is the 'appearance of the likeness'. The divine essence itself, however, remains undisclosed, hidden in the brightness of the cloud. It is the cloud of 'unknowing', as the mystics say. The knowledge of God is forever wrapped in mystery.

We may say that God is father or God is mother. At the same time, however, we must also say that God is other. God is more than anything that we can think or imagine, and certainly more than doctrinal definitions and theological understandings. As St Paul writes, 'God dwells in unapproachable light, whom no one has ever seen or can see.'[5] The Mystery can be contained by no image but only pointed to by way of analogy. The biblical tradition thus uses many names to refer to God, while recognising that none of them alone, or even all of them together, can define the Mystery. God is referred to as king and liberator, for instance, as midwife and judge, as fire and water, and as life itself. One image balances the other and throws light on the other, but always the Mystery is essentially ineffable, unutterable. As the twentieth-century kabbalist Abraham Kook says, 'All the divine names, whether Hebrew or any other language, give us only a tiny and dull spark of the hidden light to which the soul aspires when it utters the word "God".'[6]

Despite the recognition that God is beyond description, and therefore that many images must be used if we are to avoid idolising one way of seeing, there has been a tendency in our Western religious tradition to focus on one type of imagery to the exclusion of others.[7] Particularly we have allowed patriarchal imagery to dominate, with the result that God is portrayed as essentially male. This distorts our sense of the Mystery. It gives us the impression that God is somehow limited to a specific type of being, namely maleness. The image of father in the biblical tradition is not pointing to a particular gender in God. Both male and female flow forth from the mystery of God's being. Fatherhood imagery is pointing to the One from whom we have come, to God as our seed or origin of life. But as the Book of Genesis says, 'in the image of God he created them, male and female he created them'.[8] Both masculine and feminine are born from the womb of the Maker.

The earliest self-disclosure of God in the Old Testament occurs in the story of Moses encountering a bush that is on fire with the divine presence. When Moses asks by what name he is to call God, the response is 'I am who I am'.[9] The answer is not 'I am this' or 'I am that', 'I am liberator' or 'I am lord', but simply 'I am who I am'. This always is who God is. This is eternally the divine name. No matter how much we may grow in our knowledge of God as creator and redeemer, or as father or mother, the essence of God remains the same, 'I am who I am'. Everything else that we say about the Mystery needs to be said in the light of this foundational truth.

In each moment and in each place God is present to us as the One who is and who allows us to be. Without God nothing in the whole cosmos would exist, even for a second. The 'I amness' of God is the very ground of being. If taken away, all things would fall into non-existence. The great Mystery is not something that we can set alongside the mystery of our own beings or the mystery of creation's being, as if God were just one other type of being among many. God is the One through whom all things exist. Nor can we reduce the mystery of God into something that can be communicated by ideas and words. Our only true knowledge of God is our experience of God. The great twentieth-century Jewish teacher Martin Buber calls this the 'I–Thou' relationship.[10] 'Thou' is not an image to refer to God. It is the way of expressing our immediate experience of God. It is the way of giving voice to our encounter with the One who is beyond all names.

Just as the essence of God is a mystery that defies definition and can be expressed only as 'I am who I am', so the essence of each one of us is undefinable and can be expressed only as 'I am who I am'. We are made in the image of God. Therefore the mystery of our being is beyond explanation. To explain something means to make something plain, yet the roots of our being are hidden in the mystery of God's being. They are not plain to view. They stretch deep down into the invisible depths of God's mystery. No description captures these depths.

Like the fontanelle at the crown of an infant's head we are not closed in. We are like the Pantheon in Rome, the sanctuary that was designed with an opening in its roof. The building's aperture opens the sanctuary to the lights and the infinity of the skies. We too are like a temple that is open to the infinite. Our life is part of the Mystery that is greater than us. The dimensions of us that defy definition are closer to the essence of our being than any outward characteristics of our lives. As Martin Buber says, the known aspects of who we are are only 'the outside of an unknown Inward'.[11] The known and the unknown are like the two sides of a crescent moon. Our inner self is the dark and hidden side. We know of its existence but it is not visible to us. As Abraham Kook says, our inner world is 'concealed, linked to a hidden something, a world that is not our world, not yet perceived or probed'.[12]

Our deepest identity is found in these unknown dimensions of our being. Martin Buber makes a distinction between what he calls 'personhood', on the one hand, and 'individuality', on the other.[13] Personhood finds its roots in the hidden realm of God's mystery within us. Individuality finds its identity in terms of what is outwardly known and observable in our lives. Personhood says 'I am'. Individuality, on the other hand, says 'I am such and such'. These represent two poles within each of us. I can say of myself, for instance, that I am a father and a husband or that I am a blend of nationalities, Canadian and Scottish. None of these, however, captures the essence of my being. They are observable and known features of who I am, but, no matter how dear to me, they do not define my essence.

To be made in the image of God is essentially to be mystery. We may choose, of course, simply to live in terms of our outward characteristics. We may choose to view ourselves and one another primarily in terms of gender and race, for instance, or religion and vocation, but this limits us to the surface of life. It imprisons us to outward categories and to the ways in which others view and treat such

5

categories. It denies us the rich stream of unbounded mystery in which our truest identity lies. If we deny the Mystery in which we are rooted, our inner self leads a type of 'cancelled existence', says Buber, but it is forever waiting to be 'recalled'.[14] This is the longing at the heart of our lives, to be truly ourselves.

The fact that we even *are* is a marvel. It is a source of constant astonishment. The gift of conception and birth is almost unbelievable. Too often in our religious traditions we have focused so much on the gift of grace that we end up downplaying the holy gift of nature. Both are of God. We have been so conscious of our need for healing that we lose sight of the extraordinary gift of life itself. God is the Maker as well as the Remaker. Theologically, most of our attention has been directed towards the mystery of redemption without a corresponding emphasis on the mystery of creation. The Psalmist says, 'You knit me together in my mother's womb. I praise you, for I am fearfully and wonderfully made.'[15] An awareness of the gift of conception in our mother's womb should be a focal point of spirituality. It is an awareness to which we need to be recalled again and again in absolute wonder.

Something of the mystery of God's image is present in every human face. It can be glimpsed amidst the layers of meaning and experience hidden in our countenances. At times in our lives the depths of the mystery are so covered over as to have become almost entirely lost to consciousness. Yet deep in each human face is a unique reflection of the holy image, despite the great compulsions that drive us towards superficiality and conformity in our cultures. No two faces are exactly alike. As the twentieth-century Jewish teacher Abraham Heschel says, each one of us is 'an original, not a copy'.[16] There is something unprecedented in the depths of each one of us that has never been expressed before. No one can be considered average or ordinary in their place of deepest identity. It is our outwardness that conforms to sameness with others. Our inwardness is absolutely unique. It is to these inner depths that we are being recalled.

To live from the place of our unique mystery is to be a surprise, even to ourselves. Who can predict what will surge up from the unknown depths of our souls? As Abraham Heschel says, 'no person can write his autobiography in advance'.[17] Creative passions for what is just and right in our world, and deep resources to imagine and to begin again in relationship, are hidden in the inner sanctuary of our beings waiting to be set free. This is not to deny that at times we will be surprised also by layers of confusion and fear in ourselves. These also suddenly surge up from unknown recesses, whether as individuals or as whole societies, and can express themselves unpredictably in destructive and violent ways. To be recalled to the true depths of who we are is not a journey that will take us around the fearful energies that are in us but through them and into a sharper awareness of them. Deeper, however, than the forces of death in us are the springs of life, forever seeking to rise from the limitless depths of our souls.

To say that we are made in the image of God is to say that the knowledge of our true selves is linked inseparably with the knowledge of God. As the fourteenth-century English mystic Julian of Norwich sees in one of her 'Revelations of Divine Love', 'I saw no difference between God and our essence, but it was all God.' At the heart of her soul she sees Christ, entirely at home, seated on a throne. It is the boundless and everlasting kingdom of God that is within us. Only in seeking the dwelling place of God will we find our true selves. 'Our soul is so deeply founded in God,' she says, 'that we cannot acquire knowledge of it until we have knowledge of God, its creator, to whom it belongs.'[18]

In classical theological thought it has been understood that there are two paths of knowledge. These are spoken of as the *via positiva* and the *via negativa*. The positive or affirmative way of knowing the Mystery is to say that everything that has been created is an expression of God. The brilliance of the morning sun and the infinity of the night skies, the generosity of a friend and the passion of a lover's desire, the wildness of a storm and the fecundity of the earth all show something of the Creator. They are theophanies, or showings, of the Mystery. None of them, however, captures the essence of God. We can describe the expressions of the Mystery but not the Mystery itself. The negative way of knowing reminds us that God is not this and not that. God is forever more than the brilliant light of the sun and the self-giving passion of a lover. God is other than the strength of the waves of the sea and the new growth bursting forth from the dark ground.

This leads the mystics, like the ninth-century Irish teacher John Scotus Eriugena, to say that God is 'Nothing'.[19] This, of course, is not to say that God is less than anything that we can conceive of but that God is more than 'everything' that we can conceive of. Whenever we attempt to describe God, as mother or father for instance, we run the risk of thinking that God is something that we know about and can define. The essence of the Mystery is forever beyond our descriptions. As Eriugena writes in one of his prayers, 'Thou permittest to be known not what Thou art, but what Thou are not; not what Thou art, but that Thou art.'[20]

The Mystery of the Self

The *via negativa* corrects the tendency in us to think that we can describe the Mystery. God is always greater than anything we can imagine. The negative way of knowing does not deny the value of positive images of the divine. It ensures, however, that the images we use do not become idols and end up obstructing the mystery rather than shedding further light on it. In our pursuit of the knowledge of God our mind is to be like a door that opens onto what is boundless rather than like a wall that attempts to hold the mystery in. St Augustine liked to say that if we think we have understood the Mystery then what we have understood is not God but something of our own creating.

This, of course, is not to say that God is not meaning, but rather that the meaning is always enfolded by mystery. As Rabbi Heschel says, God is 'meaning that mystery alludes to'.[21] Without a regard for mystery we turn meaning into fixed forms like stone. The biblical tradition has always been alert to religion's tendency to create idols, whether of stone or of thought. Later Judaism even abstained from using the name of God, lest it be turned into a type of idol of expression. Instead it used the sacred tetragrammaton YHWH as a symbol for the holy name. The parallel in Islam is the tradition of the ninety-nine names of Allah. The hundredth is believed to be the true name but it is never pronounced because it does not exist. The mystery of God is ineffable. Only silence comes close to truly expressing the sacred mystery.

The meaning within the mystery, however, is forever seeking expression. 'My tongue lacks words . . . and I would be silent', says an eleventh-century Christian mystic, but the experience of God 'stirs up the soul and pries open my unclean mouth'.[22] We are forever torn between silence and speech, between the realisation that we cannot capture

9

in words our experience of God and the burning desire in us to try to say what is in fact unsayable. As soon as we try to put into words our sense of the Mystery we are limited by the boundaries of language and thought. As Eriugena says, what we are able to express is that God is but not what God is.

While we cannot *express* the Mystery, much more importantly we can *experience* the Mystery. God is immediately present to us in every moment of our lives. We may not be conscious of it but each one of us is constantly in contact with God. In fact, as George MacLeod, the founder of the modern-day Iona Community in Scotland, liked to say, we 'can't get out of touch with God . . . for the simple reason that God is Life; not religious life, nor Church life, but the whole life that we now live in the flesh'.[23] To have experienced life is to have experienced God. God is the Life of all life, without which nothing that is would be. The invitation is to grow into a fuller awareness of this moment-by-moment experience of Life. It is not God who is absent from us. Rather, we are absent from our true selves and from a sense of the Mystery that is at the heart of every moment.

To experience consciously the presence of God is not to have to describe God. As Martin Buber says, it is simply to be present to the experience of God, to say 'Thou' to God with our whole being. We do not have to try to turn the Mystery into an image or an idea. Even to say 'He' or 'She' about the divine is to begin to turn God into an object of thought, but not 'Thou'. 'Thou' is the utterance of our personal encounter with the Mystery. The depth of our spirituality is based not on whether or not we can say certain things *about* God but on whether or not we are aware of the presence *of* God in every moment of life and in every person we meet. At the heart of the biblical tradition is the deep yearning to be alive to God's presence, to encounter the Mystery personally and immediately.

The Bible provides us not simply with a new vision of God but with a new vision of ourselves. It tells us that we are made in the holy image and that the Holy One is not only beyond us but is within us. Bernard of Clairvaux in the twelfth century said of the divine presence, 'When I gazed out, I found it beyond all that was outside me; when I looked in, it was further in than my most inward being.'[24] It is in the deepest dimensions of who we are that we glimpse the mystery of God's presence.

To be made in the image of the Mystery is to say that we too are 'no-thing'. The essence of our being is more than any 'thing' that we know. The teachings of Jesus invite us to die to ourselves. Part of what this means is to die to the 'things' by which we define who we are and to which we cling for security. In dying to the names and definitions that obscure the mystery of our beings we are set free to be truly ourselves. Only as we know the unnameableness of who we are will we be free from the categories that hold us in bondage to external expectations. Only then will each one of us be free to be 'I am who I am', guided by what God has placed at the core of our being rather than by the preconceptions of what others define us as or think we should be. Only then will we approach a true reverence for one another and for ourselves. As Symeon the New Theologian in the eleventh century says in his prayer to God, only then will I come to 'honour and fear myself as I honour and fear thee'.[25]

We are hid within a cloud, the cloud of unknowing, but it is not a cloud of meaninglessness. It is a cloud of mystery. The Scottish poet Edwin Muir, in his poem 'The Cloud',

describes a young man harrowing in a field.[26] He is sur-
rounded by a haze of dust. Everything, says Muir, seems
'encrusted with a hard sheath of dust' and the young man
appears to be nothing but 'a pillar of dust moving in dust'.
It is a picture of barren meaninglessness. In contrast with
the biblical picture of the burning bush alive with God's
presence and the pillar of flame guiding Israel through the
wilderness, Muir describes the bushes as dry and everything as lifeless. Even the human form seems merely 'dust
made sublime by dust'. Muir longs for 'light to break' so
that he can see again 'the face once broken in Eden'. It is,
he says, the 'world-without-end lamented face'. It may be a
broken face, buried under layers of confusion and wrongdoing, but it is there within each one of us waiting to be
restored.

Our true face, as Muir says in his autobiography, is an
immortal mystery:

> We extend far beyond any boundary line which we can
> set for ourselves in the past or the future. . . . I know my
> name, the date and place of my birth, the appearance of
> the places I have lived in, the people I have met, the
> things I have done. I know something of the society
> which dictates many of my actions, thoughts, and feel-
> ings. I know a little about history, and can explain it to
> myself in rough-and-ready fashion how that society
> came into being. But . . . if I knew all these figures and
> names I should still not know myself, far less all the
> other people in the world, or the small number whom
> I call friends. This external approach, no matter how
> perfect, will never teach me much either about them or
> about myself.[27]

This leads Muir towards another type of knowing, into what he calls 'moments of contemplation' which include dreams and daydreams. In these moments of 'self-forgetfulness', as he calls them, there issues up from the subconscious a sense of the mystery and the immortality of our beings. 'Sleep', he says, 'tells us things about ourselves and the world which we could not discover otherwise.' Such moments provide us with 'glints of immortality'.[28]

The kabbalistic tradition says that 'a dream that is not interpreted is like a letter that is not read'.[29] No dimension of our lives should be excluded from the practice of listening for the Mystery, for God is the Life of all life. In the Old Testament there are many instances of divine disclosure and guidance offered through dreams. Angels of God visit people in the night and speak to them in the stillness of their sleep. As the Book of Job says, God speaks in more than one way, 'though people do not perceive it. In a dream, in a vision of the night, when deep sleep falls on mortals, while they slumber on their beds, then he opens their ears.'[30] In the New Testament it is wise men attentive to dreams and to the movement of the stars who are guided to the Christ-child, just as it is responsiveness to dream life that protects the new-born child from Herod's slaughter of the innocents.[31] Given the essential undefinableness of God and the unbounded reality of what is at the heart of our lives, it is the rich realm of the subconscious issuing up in our dream life and in moments of stillness and contemplation that will come closest to communicating the ineffable mystery of God to us.

But how are we to be guided in our interpretations of the subconscious and in our listening for the mystery of God in all things? How do we discern truth amidst what can feel like a flood of images and stirrings of new consciousness within us? It is easy to deceive ourselves in the search for new perceptions and directions in our lives and relationships. What is the yardstick by which we measure the intimations that well up from the depths of our being?

Eriugena calls Christ 'our epiphany'.[32] This is to say that Christ is not only the epiphany of God, 'the Word made flesh' as St John says,[33] but that he is *our* epiphany. He manifests what is deepest in us, made as we are in the image of God. Christ is 'the image of the invisible God', says St Paul.[34] He perfectly reflects the mystery of God's being to us, as well as the mystery of our own being. In Christ we see the face of God. In him we see also our true face.

So distant have we become from what is deepest in us that we will not know the depths of our being unless we are shown them. Christ's conception and birth, and his dying and rising, are an epiphany of the true nature of our beings. The truth of who we are is 'hid with Christ in God', as St Paul says.[35] The gospel is given not to tell us what we already know about ourselves, but rather to tell us what we do not know, or what we have forgotten, namely who we are. It is given to lead us into the true depths of the mystery of God's image within us.

Christ's conception by the Holy Spirit points to what is true of the gift of life itself. In the beginning all things were conceived by the Spirit in the virgin womb of the universe. The Genesis picture is of the Spirit hovering over the primeval waters. This is an image of the genesis of all things. It speaks also of what is deepest and most original in each one of us. The mystery of our beings, boundless and undefinable, is conceived by the Spirit. We are born of flesh and matter. We come into being through those who have gone before us. Like the earth our bodies are born and will die, but the essence of our being is of the eternal mystery of God.

Jesus, as the embodiment of the Mystery, refuses to define himself. He speaks of himself only as 'Son of Man', which is neither a name nor a title. No one else in the Scriptures uses the term to refer to him and no one objects to it being used by Jesus. In fact no one questions it at all or shows any kind of reaction to it. Similarly, after the New Testament it never features in any of the confessions of faith. In Galilee the term 'Son of Man' was used simply as a circumlocution for oneself. Instead of saying 'I', Jesus says 'Son of Man'. It was also a synonym for 'human being'. For Jesus to say that 'the Son of Man is lord of the sabbath' was another way of saying, as Jesus did say, that 'the sabbath was made for humankind and not humankind for the sabbath'.[36] Throughout his life Jesus points not only to the mystery at the heart of his own being but to the unnameable mystery at the heart of every human being. He leads us into the truth of our deepest identity.

In his trial before the Roman governor of Palestine we find the same determination in Jesus not to be bound by titles. In response to Pilate's question, 'Are you the King of the Jews?', he replies, 'So you say'. Similarly when he is accused by the chief priests and elders of religion, he refuses to answer. St Matthew records how Pilate pursues the issue again with Jesus. 'But he gave him no answer', says Matthew, and 'the governor was greatly amazed'. The Gospel account conveys the sense of frustration that was felt at Jesus' refusal to define himself or to defend himself. It is the frustration that has been experienced again and again through the centuries when mystics, for instance, have refused to label the divine mystery with recognisably orthodox titles or to place neat boundaries around the central convictions of their spiritual tradition.

In the Gospel story it is a frustration that is as irksome to the state as it is to religion. Their response is mockery and violence. The religious say, 'Crucify him'. The soldiers of the state place a scarlet robe and crown of thorns on him. They then 'spat on Jesus', writes Matthew, 'and struck him on the head'.[37]

What is it in our traditions that has felt so uncomfortable about sitting with mystery, and at times reacts so angrily to those who refuse to be strait-jacketed by the tight boundaries of religious definitions? The frenzy of different forms of fundamentalism in our world speaks of the fear that surfaces in us when it becomes clear that the Mystery cannot be controlled but only adored.

The crown of the head represents the place of mystery. To be beaten over the head, as Jesus was, speaks of a violation of the Mystery. It is the sort of blasphemy that we witness and experience in our world when a reverence for the other is lost. Only when we have ceased to address one another as 'thou' can we so act towards another human being. Only when we have labelled others in terms of race and gender, or religion and class, can we move towards being able to turn them into objects and strike against the sacred mystery of their being.

In the biblical tradition the head is reverenced. St John the Divine, for instance, sees an angel of God wrapped in cloud 'with a rainbow over his head', an image of mystery and promise. The Son of Man is pictured with 'a golden crown on his head' and the woman clothed in the sun is crowned with stars.[38] These symbols speak not only of a type of royal lineage that is bestowed upon the image of God, the belief that we have been 'crowned with glory and honour' as the Psalmist says,[39] but of a type of boundlessness to the mystery of our beings, crowned with the infinity of the heavens.

In the Book of Revelation, however, the head can also be a place of perverted mystery. There are the creatures that issue up out of the shaft of the bottomless pit. Emerging out of the smoke 'their faces were like human faces', writes St John, 'their hair like women's hair, and their teeth like lions' teeth'. 'On their heads', he says, 'were what looked like crowns of gold.'[40] This is a picture of the way in which evil can masquerade as mystery. At heart, however, it is unnatural. It is a perversion of what is mostly deeply planted within us. Rather than the cloud of mystery it is the 'smoke' of evil deceiving us with its apparent resemblance to mystery. The 'great red dragon' of the Book of Revelation even manifests a multiplication of heads and of diadems on its many crowns.[41] The seemingly limitless depths of evil's resources can mesmerise and captivate us as individuals and as whole nations. The cloud of divine mystery and the smoke of evil, of course, are not simply outside of us. They reflect also the inner dimensions of the divine mystery and the capacity for evil that are within the soul of every human being. As William Blake puts it, there are 'Two Limits' in the soul of humanity. 'In every Human bosom those Limits stand.'[42]

No matter how far into the mystery we move it is not exhausted. Regardless of how much we come to know about God and about ourselves the mystery remains infinite. To say that Christ is the perfect embodiment of God is not to say that the mystery has been displaced by knowledge. Rather, the self-disclosure of God in Christ leads us into a deepened perception of God as mystery. In the story of the transfiguration, when the brilliance of the divine presence is glimpsed in Jesus and 'his face shone like the sun', as St Matthew says, the voice that names Christ as 'the Beloved' and that calls the disciples to 'listen to him' is uttered from within the cloud of brightness.[43] It is the cloud of unknowing. We are invited into a closer knowing of God but not in a way that lessens God's mystery. We move towards a fuller awareness of God but not towards a dispelling of the bright cloud. We cannot translate the mystery of our encounter with God into words. Mystery is at the very heart of our relationship with God in Christ. As the twentieth-century theologian Hans Urs von Balthasar put it, 'the mystery of divine incomprehensibility burns more brightly here than anywhere'.[44] Christ leads us into a sharper sense of the Mystery.

How then do we grow in a knowledge of God's mystery? It is not, as we have noted, through a knowledge *about* God but only through a knowledge *of* God. We come to know the Mystery more and more only through a direct and personal awareness of God's presence. At the heart of the Christian epiphany is the belief that above all else the mystery of God is a mystery of love. 'God is love', as St John says, 'and those who live in love live in God, and God lives in them.'[45] As the nineteenth-century Indian teacher Ramakrishna says, 'Knowledge has entry only up to the outer rooms of God.' Only love can enter God's 'most secret chambers'.[46] It is only through love that we will know God, just as it is only through love that we will truly know one another. It is the love, as St Paul says, 'that surpasses knowledge'.[47]

Words for Meditation

'You anoint my head with oil' *(Psalm 23:5)*.

18

2

THE WISDOM OF THE SELF

The forehead represents the place of wisdom. We are familiar, especially from the East, with the idea of the third eye or the inner eye, symbolised in Hinduism by the red dot in the middle of the forehead. It speaks of a way of perceiving that is deeper than outward sight. But equally the closed or hardened forehead can symbolise a denial of wisdom. The Prophecy of Isaiah uses the image of a forehead like 'brass' to represent obstinacy and a refusal to see and to know.[1]

Ecclesiasticus says that wisdom was made with us in the womb.[2] It is part of the image of God in which we are made. It is at the core of the mystery of our being. Similarly, St Paul says that truth has been inscribed into our inner being.[3] Redemption in part is about being reconnected to this wisdom within.

Edwin Muir, in his poem 'Day and Night', speaks of things that we know 'yet never have been told'.[4] He is pointing to a type of intuitive wisdom that has been planted deep within us. He contrasts the day's way of seeing with the night's way. The perceptions of the day are learned and analytical. In the day we see life in its parts. The night's way of seeing, on the other hand, is intuitive. It perceives things in their unity and at levels deeper than thought. As a child, he says, it was from the night that he first discovered the ancient or the unitive way of seeing. 'The night, the night alone is old,' he says, 'and showed me only what I knew, knew, yet never had been told.' It is a way of perceiving that emerges out of our inner being. Its speech is 'too deep for daily tongues to say', and it rises into our consciousness in 'unexplained simplicity', says Muir.

This is similar to what many of the mystics have wanted to say about the way of unknowing. Symeon the New Theologian in the eleventh century said that wisdom sees what is 'altogether simple'.[5] It is in fact too simple for words. True wisdom is not too complex for words. Rather it is too simple for expression. And as well as being 'simple', says Muir, it is 'natural'. It issues up from our place of deepest natural origin, which for Muir is represented by the Garden of Eden. Muir, of course, is not saying that we are to choose the night's way of seeing over and against the day's way. We need the night and the day, the mystical and intuitive as well as the intellectual and rational. 'I would have them both,' he says, 'would nothing miss, learn from the shepherd of the dark, here in the light.'

A predominant theme throughout Muir's writings is the reconnection with childhood's way of knowing. There is the mythical Jewish saying that in our mother's wombs we know God, but at birth we begin to forget. It is in the dark hours of the night, during sleep and in the stillness of contemplation and prayer, that we come closest to that way of knowing again.

In America I was once told the story of a little girl and her baby brother. When the baby boy was born the girl kept asking her parents if she could spend time alone with her newborn brother. The parents finally agreed, and intrigued by why she was making this request they listened at the door. The little girl said to her baby brother, 'Tell me what God is like. I'm beginning to forget.'

This is similar to William Blake's story from childhood of seeing a tree full of angels. Upon telling his father about the angels of light, however, he was warned that if he repeated such lies again he would be beaten. For Edwin Muir, in fact, this is precisely when our loss of natural wisdom begins to occur. It happens when we no longer allow ourselves, or when we are no longer allowed, to see things with our own eyes. He describes this process in his own boyhood:

> I had lost my first clear vision of the world, and reached the stage when a child tries desperately to see things as his elders see them, and hopes to grow up by pretending to be grown up . . . Under that compulsion I could not see things with my own eyes; instead I tried to see them as I thought my father and my mother . . . saw them. I eagerly falsified them, knowing that the falsification was expected by every one: my parents, my teachers, visitors to the house, even other boys, who were enthusiastically doing the very thing that I was doing . . . It is in these years between eleven and eighteen that we construct little by little, with the approval of all the world, the mask which we shall wear with such ease when we reach manhood, feeling then that we were born with it, though it is merely a face which was made to look like a face by our own clumsy hands at an age when we did not know what we were doing.[6]

Muir's memory is of a personal loss of innocence. It is accompanied by a suppression of wisdom in its childlike simplicity.

The Genesis version is similarly of a loss of innocence

that comes with the knowledge of good and evil.[7] The biblical story points to the way in which we become aware of the opposites latent in creation and in ourselves. We become alert to our capacity for good and evil, or to what Martin Buber calls the 'yes-position' to life and the 'no-position' to life.[8] Once we come to know of the choice between good and evil, then a tension of oppositeness characterises our lives. This does not mean that we will always choose evil, or that we are incapable of choosing good, as the doctrine of original sin suggests, but that we will always have the choice of choosing evil.

What Scripture refers to as 'the imagination of the human heart'[9] is the way in which we play with the possibilities of how we will use our knowledge. Once we know what can be done in our relationships and with our power and sexuality, for instance, then there is always the possibility that we may choose evil. The story of Cain deciding to kill his brother Abel is the first example of how the knowledge of good and evil can work itself out. Cain becomes a 'wanderer' on the earth, a 'fugitive' from his true self and from the wisdom with which he was born. His outward wandering is merely a reflection of the inner exile that has already occurred.

The Genesis account of humanity expelled from the Garden and wandering the earth is continually repeated in the human story. It also reflects what happens in our own individual lives. We become fugitives from the wisdom that has been planted deep within us. The passage into adolescence, as Edwin Muir refers to in his autobiography, can be a time of tremendous transition in relation to the knowledge of good and evil. The possibilities of what we may do with our minds and bodies and energies break upon us with staggering force.

The Wisdom of the Self

Throughout my own adolescence I had a recurring dream in which I would find myself reading an ancient manuscript. It was an image of something like a perennial wisdom that I had access to. But as soon as I became aware in the dream that I was reading, the ancient manuscript would become illegible to me. It was as if the script had become a foreign language that I no longer understood. The dream speaks of the way in which as adolescents our acquired ways of knowing, including the educating of our intellect and reason, can begin to block the deeper ability to read from the eternal script of wisdom within ourselves.

As William Blake says, our 'Visions of Eternity' become weak through a narrowing of our perceptions. In 'Visions of the Daughters of Albion' he writes:

> They told me that the night & day were all that I could see; They told me that I had five senses to inclose me up. And they inclos'd my infinite brain into a narrow circle.[10]

Instead of glimpsing 'the depths of wondrous worlds' within ourselves, our eye has become 'a little narrow orb', he says, 'closd up & dark, scarcely beholding the Great Light'.[11]

We become 'obscure texts' to ourselves, as Rabbi Heschel says.[12] We hardly even know the alphabet of the inner language of ancient wisdom that has been written into us. We are like messengers who have forgotten the message, and to forget the message that has been etched into our beings is to become disorientated and eventually mad. Blake's image is of a type of 'fever of the human soul'. Elsewhere he calls it 'a reflexion of Eden all perverted'.[13]

Edwin Muir writes in his autobiography, 'I felt that I had

gone far away from myself.' To live at a distance from the centre of our being is to feel cut off from ourselves as well as alienated from one another. In describing his early years of adulthood, Muir writes, 'Something in myself was buried, and I was only half there as I worked in the office and wandered about the roads.' Not only is it an exile from himself and other human beings. The world itself, he says, 'retreated from me with all its shapes'.[14] Like Cain in the Genesis account, Muir becomes a fugitive from his inner self and from the whole of life. The result is that he begins to seek company with 'desperate eagerness', as he says. 'I was more sociable and more lonely than I had ever been before.'[15] His words describe the way in which if we are not at home with ourselves we will not be at home with anyone.

What is it that reconnects us to home or to 'Eden', that deepest dimension of who we are but from which we have become distant? Jesus says, 'Unless you change and become like children, you will never enter the kingdom of heaven.'[16] One man, in meditating on the theme of wisdom saw a little boy on a path beckoning to him, and then realised that the little boy was in fact himself. The child within himself was calling him to return. Similarly, another person in meditation saw a heavy dark wooden door standing slightly ajar. Through the opening he could see his children playing in a garden. There were other children too, some of whom he recognised as adult friends of his who in the meditation had become children. He decided to enter the garden to be with them and to play. After a while he saw that he too had become a child again.

These images of recovering the child within ourselves, like Jesus' words about becoming a child in order to enter the kingdom of heaven, are not romanticising childhood.

Rather, they are speaking about our need to be changed, radically. They are calling us to be reconnected to something deep within us. It is not suggesting an idyllic return to the innocent wisdom of infancy, for even if we wished to we could not return to that place. God's holy and natural gift of conception and life, in which wisdom was born with us in the womb, is now wounded and marred in our lives in all sorts of ways. We are not simply looking to nature for our salvation, but neither are we to be looking simply to grace. Both nature and grace are gifts of God. The gift of grace is given to work a mystery of resurrection in our lives, to recover the wisdom that has been planted at the heart of our human nature.

To say that wisdom is born with us in the womb is not to pretend that we do not need the gift of grace. Rather it is to say that the gift of grace is given to heal something deep within us that has become broken. It is given not to make us something other than ourselves, but to make us truly ourselves. It is given not to connect us to something outside of us but to reunite us to something at the very core of our beings.

What is the path towards such a recovery of wisdom? Ecclesiasticus, in saying that wisdom is born with us in the womb, immediately goes on to say that 'to fear God is the beginning of wisdom', or to fear God is to begin to recover wisdom.[17] By 'fear' is not meant a cowering timidity, a characteristic that religion at times has attempted to engender in us. Rather the fear of God is an attitude of awe, or, as Rabbi Heschel says, of 'radical amazement' at life and its mysteries, like that of a child's.[18] The Book of Proverbs in fact describes wisdom as a 'little child' who 'delights' in life.[19] Open-eyed amazement is a way of understanding. It is a way of seeing, and if we have lost radical amazement at life then we will not truly see life. We need to die to acquired and complacent ways of seeing if we are to regain the open-eyed wonder at life that was ours in infancy, the almost unbelievableness of every moment.

Edwin Muir's experience of grace happens in part through an attentiveness to his dream life. A number of his recorded dreams call him to let go to the depths that are within him. Recounting one of his London dreams he writes:

I was in a wild, rocky place, treeless and shrubless, and in the midst of it I came to an enormous white palace. The walls were high and windowless, and there was only one small door. I went up to it and pushed. The door opened at once, but when I took my hand away shut again, and would not open a second time. Then I saw a small opening, about three feet square, just beside the door. Creeping through it, I stepped on to the balcony of a great hall. Looking up, I could see the roof far above me; but downward the hall went farther than my eyes could follow, and seemed to sink deep into the ground. This lower part was covered with wooden scaffoldings, and was obviously under repair, though no workmen could be seen; the place seemed to have been deserted for a long time. I climbed on to the balustrade, raised my hands above my head, and dived. I had fallen head downward for a great distance, when my hand caught a beam of one of the scaffoldings, and I began to climb upward again, hand over hand, at a great speed, with the ease of an ape. I did not stop until my head was touching the ceiling and I could go no farther. Again I was filled with rage. I beat my head against the ceiling, which was thick and decorated with fine mouldings, and broke through it. Above, there was a broad terrace lined with cypresses; night had fallen, and the dark blue sky was glittering with stars.[20]

The dream provides a picture of Muir diving into the fathomless depths of his soul, which he sees as a white palace. He has been distant from it, wandering in a barren place. In order to enter the palace of his soul he needs to pass through what is like the 'narrow gate' of Jesus' parable.[21] He has to bend down to enter. Upon entering he finds that it is of immeasurable depth. He sees that it has been deserted for a long time and is in need of repair. It is at this point that he decides to dive into the depths. Only in letting go to the boundless depths of his being does he become aware also that the heights of his being have been artificially enclosed. With his head, the symbol of mystery and wisdom, he breaks through the ceiling. Instead of the wilderness in which he has been wandering there are now trees growing under an infinity of night sky.

It is a picture of discovering the 'glittering' freedom of the heights of our being, but only after giving ourselves to the depths, of diving with a type of reckless abandon into the boundless foundations of the palace of our souls. Letting go to the depths of our being releases in us new ways of seeing. The new seeing, however, does not come out of nothing. As Abraham Kook says, we are like coal that, set alight, releases the energy that was stored in it at the time of its formation.[22] New ways of seeing come forth from the wisdom that was formed within us in our mother's womb. It needs to be transferred up into the light of our understanding. There are 'hidden things that you have not known', as Isaiah says.[23] It is from these depths that we can draw ways of seeing that have never been known before.

New understanding then is something that comes forth from the inner riches of wisdom's deposit in us. The Jewish kabbalists, very much like Edwin Muir, believed that understanding has its original root in Eden. True perception issues up from the deepest part of who we are, from the place of our origin or genesis in God. As a tenth-century Indian mystic said, the gifts of wisdom are like shells that lie in the sea of our hearts. Enlightenment is when they are cast up onto the shore of our consciousness and spring open.[24] Blake's image is of an inner garden that has been 'Planted & Sown' long before we were born.[25] There is a treasure in the field of our beings, the depths of which we cannot conceive, yet everything we truly need is already there.

The seeds of wisdom impregnate our understanding. They give birth to what the kabbalists called 'new-ancient words',[26] new and creative perceptions that never before have been expressed but which have their root in the eternal wisdom that resides deep within us. As Jesus says, the teacher who has been 'trained for the kingdom of heaven is like the master of a household who brings out of his treasure what is new and what is old'. [27] This is one of the marks of wisdom's treasure. It is forever new and forever ancient.

One of the true marks of wisdom therefore is humility, for although the wise may give voice to insights that have never been expressed, they know that the wellspring of wisdom is deeper than them and is pure gift. It is an everlasting stream flowing through them in new ways. And so, as Ecclesiasticus says, 'honour yourself with humility'.[28] Again it needs to be said that humility is not a demeaning of the self, and certainly not a self-hatred. Humility is a returning to oneself, to the root or earth (*humus*) of one's being. Humility is about being reconnected to the ground of our soul. It is what Rabbi Kook calls a 'noble humility'.[29]

In another Muir dream there is again a type of diving into the depths. This time it is a diving into the ground of his being. In the dream he sees himself millions of miles from the earth in a padded cell. The imagery is of being distant and 'cushioned' from life as well as from his true depths. Again he finds a small opening, this time a window, and crawls out on to the sill. The earth far beneath him is covered in cloud but he has 'an overpowering longing to be down there'. He lifts his hands over his head and dives. When he catches sight of the earth he sees that it is 'completely covered with ice'. It is an image of his depths frozen over, like Blake's image of the gates that lead to Eden as frozen shut.[30] He realises that he is going to be 'broken to pieces' by the fall. He sees himself striking the ice and 'lying outspread and shattered'. Then he writes:

> After a while a black, smooth-skinned animal somewhat like a walrus, but much bigger, came out of a hole in the ice, went over to my body, and sniffed it. The great beast looked sad and kindly, but after sniffing my body ate it up in a businesslike way and went back into the hole again. I waited still . . . for I knew that something else would happen. And after a while I saw myself coming out of the hole, reborn, with a sun-coloured serpent wrapped round my breast, its head resting on my shoulder. As I walked on, new grass sprang under my feet and on either side of me.[31]

This is a dream that speaks of the cost of being reconnected to the ground, the *humus*, of our being. It is a journey that will take us through a type of dying in order to live, a dying to the falseness of what we have become or a dying to the ways in which we have become distant from the ground of our being and of all being.

In falling into the depths of our souls, and in letting our ways of thinking and seeing be shattered by such a fall, only then will we be opened to the possibility of wisdom's resurrection in us. In meditating on this theme one woman heard within herself the words, 'The wisdom is there, child. The wisdom is there.' The words encouraged her to let go to the depths. As the Jewish mystics say, 'more than the calf wants to suck the cow wants to suckle'.[32] Even more than we long for wisdom, God longs to restore us to our inner treasure of wisdom.

The way of humility of course is not simply a reverencing of our *own* depths but of what is at the ground of *all* life and of *every* life. A knowledge that is not rooted in humility becomes a manipulation of knowledge for one's own ends. It serves one's own ethnic group and religious community or one's own species over and against the rest of creation. We see this and experience it in our relationships as individuals and as nations, as well as in our collective relationship with the environment. Knowledge without humility is an attempt to try to possess the power of truth for our own exclusive blessing with a disregard to the rest of life.

True wisdom also gives rise to a different way of teaching, a different relationship between the teacher and the one who is taught. The role of the teacher is not to bestow wisdom, from on high as it were, but to release it from within. As Abraham Kook says, it is 'to draw on what is hidden in the heart' of the pupil.[33] It is not that as teachers we possess wisdom and others do not. Rather, our role is to set free the wisdom that is already within them, perhaps buried under layers of ice. Similarly, we cannot open their eyes for them but we can help them see for themselves. It is for this reason that the Jewish holy men, the *tzaddikim*, did not teach from pulpits. They taught not from above their hearers but on the same level as them, in the marketplaces and in the meadows.

Jesus says, 'Woe to you lawyers! For you have taken away the key of knowledge; you did not enter yourselves, and you hindered those who were entering.'[34] The key of knowledge is faith, the faith that wisdom is deep within us, the faith that we are made in the image of God. Jesus criticises the religious authorities for their depending excessively on law instead of entering the treasure house of wisdom themselves, but especially he criticises them for trying to prevent others from entering. Is this not the way in which we as religious traditions often have hindered people from exploring the depths of their inner life, by teaching them to distrust what is at the heart of their being rather than to believe that deeper than any confusions in them is the truth of what God has inscribed into their hearts?

Jesus taught with parables, which nearly always end with a type of question. As Jesus says at the end of his 'Good Samaritan' parable, 'Which of these three, do you think, was a neighbour to the man who fell into the hands of the robbers?'[35] He invites his listeners to uncover the truth about life for themselves. As St Matthew says, 'without a parable he told them nothing'.[36] Similarly St Luke records Jesus asking his hearers, 'Why do you not judge for yourselves what is right?'[37] Elsewhere, Jesus says to the Pharisees, don't go looking here and there for the coming of God; 'the kingdom of God is within you'.[38] In the same way the prophet Isaiah had assured the people that their Teacher would not be hidden from them, 'When you turn to the right or when you turn to the left, your ears shall hear a word within you, saying, "This is the way; walk in it."'[39] As Symeon the New Theologian says in one of his prayers, 'Never has thou hidden thyself from anyone; it is we who hide ourselves from thee.'[40]

In the Celtic tradition there is the fourth-century story of Pelagius being asked by a young woman for a rule of life. She was considering a contemplative vocation. It is said that Pelagius wrote back to her saying: 'Don't ask me! You need to discover what is written on your heart. Learn to read there what God has inscribed into your very being. Once you have read within yourself what you are being called to be, then write it out on a piece of paper and allow that to become your rule of life. But, after you have put into writing what you have read in your heart, compare what you have written with God's perfect expression, Christ the Word made flesh. If there is discrepancy between what you read in Christ and what you read in your heart, know that you have misread your heart. Then go back and read again.'

This is an important story, for it conveys the Christian belief that Christ is the yardstick by which we measure the truth of what we read in our inner beings. We are not left merely to the subjectivity of the inner soundings of our hearts. We can compare what we hear within ourselves to the Word that has been uttered in the mystery of Christ. But the story also conveys the Celtic conviction that the Word heard in Christ is not an utterance that is foreign to us. We may have become foreign to it, but it is the truth that has been etched into our very beings. Christ gives expression to what God has placed deep within us. As Eriugena says, Christ is 'our epiphany'. He shows us our true self.

The Wisdom of the Self

There is the Gospel story of people being puzzled by Jesus' wisdom. 'How does this man have such learning, when he has never been taught?', they ask.[41] And as St Matthew writes, 'the crowds were astounded at his teaching, for he taught them as one having authority, and not as their scribes'.[42] The scribes were people of immense learning, of much greater 'learning' than Jesus, but this did not mean that their authority was not to be challenged. Jesus can be found repeatedly saying to his listeners, 'You have heard that it was said . . . But I say to you . . . You have heard that it was said, "You shall love your neighbour and hate your enemy." But I say to you, Love your enemies and pray for those who persecute you.'[43]

As the New Testament scholar, the South African Dominican Albert Nolan, writes, Jesus 'did not make authority his truth, he made truth his authority'.[44] He does not expect his listeners to obey *him* but to obey the *truth* of what he is teaching. He appeals to the wisdom that has been planted within their hearts. 'Judge for yourselves,' he says. The astonishment among his hearers is not simply at the authority of Jesus but the realisation, as St Matthew writes, that 'such authority has been given to human beings'.[45] And because Jesus speaks from the place of inner wisdom and encourages others to enter that place for themselves, the Pharisees and those who choose not to enter take offence at him. They begin to try to eliminate him, as religious authorities often do when they feel threatened by an appeal to inner wisdom instead of to external deposits of truth which they think they control.

The Prophecy of Isaiah says, 'I will give you the treasures of darkness and riches hidden in secret places.'[46] How do we access these inner riches of wisdom? As St Paul says, God's wisdom is 'secret and hidden'.[47] To pursue the hidden and secret utterances of the soul we need to develop ways of listening, practices of solitude so that we can be attentive to the promptings of wisdom that issue up from these depths. 'You need to increase aloneness,' says Rabbi Kook, 'liberation of mind, until finally your soul reveals itself to you, spangling a few sparkles of her lights.'[48]

Withdrawing into silence and contemplative solitude is not a moving away from life but rather an approaching of the One who is Life, in order to reflect more deeply on the life of the world. It is not a discarding of our human experiences and engagement in life and relationships but a distilling of our joys and struggles. As Abraham Heschel says, 'Genuine solitude is a search for genuine solidarity.'[49]

The challenge for us in the modern Western world in withdrawing into solitude is that there is much in us that has become closed off. Our depths of wisdom are like wells that have been clogged up. They are like the wells of Genesis 26 of which it is written, 'the Philistines shut them and filled them with earth'. In the Genesis story the picture of Isaac digging again the wells that had been dug in the days of his ancestors is an image of releasing again the flow of wisdom from our inner beings.

The biblical tradition speaks of ways and disciplines by which the wisdom that is within us is to be sought. The Book of Wisdom, for instance, says that we are to 'rise early to meet her' and to pray 'at the dawning of the light'.[50] This was Jesus' practice, of getting up early in the morning 'while it was still very dark' and withdrawing to places of solitude.[51] Interestingly, in the Gospel texts the models for contemplation, apart from Jesus, are women. There is Mary the mother of Jesus 'pondering' in her heart, and Mary of Bethany 'listening' at Jesus' feet.[52]

In the biblical tradition wisdom in fact *is* feminine. She is from the very beginning, says Proverbs, even 'before the mountains had been shaped' and is everywhere present.[53] She can be found 'sitting at the gate', as the Book of Wisdom says, that is at the very gateway of our souls waiting to be met.[54] 'At the entrance of the portals she cries out' and her cry, say the Scriptures, is 'to all that live'. Her message is of 'life' and her warnings are of 'death'.[55]

In Jewish tradition she is described as a ravishingly beautiful woman living deep in the palace of our souls. Every day she calls out inviting us into her dwelling. At first she opens just the smallest of windows to reveal her face to us. Her brief disclosures awaken awareness and longings in us. Only if we hover daily around the gateway of our souls will wisdom show more and more of herself to us, telling us secrets that have been hidden since the foundations of the world.

In the biblical tradition, of course, it is not just a wise woman that sits at the gateway of our souls. There is also the 'foolish woman', says Proverbs.[56] Her voice is loud and her words are cheap. We need to be discerning about what we hear at the gateway of our souls. We need also to help one another unravel and interpret what we hear. The intimations from wisdom's palace may seem strange to us but we need to be uninhibited in trying to express the 'secrets'. Her riches are boundless. Sometimes we have been given the impression in our religious traditions that everything has already been said. It has all been sown up and defined. The reality is that there are ways of seeing and thinking that we do not yet know about. As the Prophecy of Isaiah says, 'new things I now declare' to you.[57] God is forever declaring new depths of the mystery from the heart of life. Only as we share openly with one another the fragments of the 'new-ancient words' that we read within ourselves will fresh perceptions of truth emerge among us and between us in the world. 'The multitude of the wise', says the Book of Wisdom, 'is the salvation of the world.'[58]

Just as it is taught in the Old Testament that wisdom sets 'free the imprisoned soul',[59] so Jesus taught that it is the truth that will set us free.[60] 'For this I was born,' he says, 'and for this I came into the world, to testify to the truth.'[61] The early Christian tradition identified Christ as the one upon whom 'the Spirit of wisdom and understanding' rested.[62] Rapidly the Church moved from simply under-standing Jesus as the messenger of Sophia towards also see-ing him as the embodiment of Sophia. As St Paul says, 'Christ . . . the wisdom of God'.[63] Similarly, in the early centuries churches are dedicated to Christ under the title *Hagia Sophia* ('Holy Wisdom'). A distinction is made, however, between Christ's wisdom and the 'wisdom of this age', as St Paul calls it.[64] Christ's wisdom in fact appears 'foolishness' to this age.[65] As Jesus himself had said, wisdom is hidden from the so-called 'wise' and is revealed to 'infants'.[66] Also wisdom's source is not primarily from without, through the recognised and respectable channels of learning and tradition, but from within, through the uncontrollable flow of 'the Spirit', the Spirit that searches everything 'even the depths of God'.[67]

'The treasure of wisdom and knowledge' that is hidden in Christ, as St Paul says,[68] is the treasure that is hidden in the depths of life itself waiting to be released. Christ is the life of the world. His wisdom is not an esoteric knowledge for the initiated few out on the religious edge of life. It is the expression of the wisdom that is deep in the image of God at the heart of every life. The mystery of Christ's crucifix-ion and resurrection points to the way in which wisdom is crucified in our lives and in the relationships of our world.

It points also to the promise of wisdom's ultimate victory over foolishness. This is the type of victory that someone like Desmond Tutu saw would come in South Africa. He saw it long before the collapse of apartheid, a goodness stronger than evil, a truth stronger than falsehood.

Edwin Muir provides us with a personal glimpse of the resurrection of wisdom in the midst of the foolishness and pain of our lives. In February 1939, as the world was preparing for war, and as Muir's wife was ill in hospital, he began to hear a truth that had been long forgotten in his life. It was rising again from within him, and he saw that it was a truth that was forever rising from the heart of life. He wrote in his diary:

> Last night, going to bed alone, I suddenly found myself ... reciting the Lord's Prayer in a loud, emphatic voice – a thing I had not done for many years – with deep urgency and profound disturbed emotion. While I went on I grew more composed; as if it had been empty and craving and were being replenished, my soul grew still; every word had a strange fullness of meaning which astonished and delighted me. It was late; I had sat up reading; I was sleepy; but as I stood in the middle of the floor half-undressed, saying the prayer over and over, meaning after meaning sprang from it, overcoming me again with joyful surprise; and I realized that this simple petition was always universal and always inexhaustible, and day by day was renewing human life.[69]

This is a story of how from unknown depths Christ's wisdom rises again within us, having been long dead. It is, as Blake says, 'the most Ancient, the Eternal and the Everlasting Gospel'.[70] Christ reveals not a new truth but the ancient, eternal truth that has been forgotten. It is the truth newly revealed. God's grace of redemption is not opposed to God's gift of creation. Grace is given to restore us to our true naturalness.

The wisdom, or the truth, that Jesus comes to reveal is not simply for the salvation of individuals or for part of the world but for the whole of life. As Proverbs says, wisdom 'rejoices' in the whole of creation. She 'delights' in the entire human race and her path includes the way of 'justice'.[71] The commandment to love God with our whole mind, and thus be restored in wisdom, is linked inseparably with the commandment to love our neighbour as ourselves.[72] The rediscovery of wisdom in our depths is not an end in itself. It is given to serve the mystery of love. The opening of 'eyes that are blind', as Isaiah says, is held together with the liberating of 'prisoners from the dungeon'.[73] The redemption of wisdom is for the redemption of the world.

There is the story of the Hasidic master who said that when he wanted to look at things in particular he needed to put his spectacles on because otherwise he would see things with his inner eyes which is to see everything as one. Wisdom sees all things not in separateness but in unity. The recovery of wisdom in our own lives is part of the healing of the world.

Words for Meditation

'Show me wisdom in my inner being' *(Psalm 51:6).*

3

THE STRENGTH OF THE SELF

The arms of the human body represent strength. The left arm is associated with the strength of power and the right arm with the strength of love. The greatest of strengths is love, greater than any power. To be made in the image of God is to be 'endowed with strength like God's own', as Ecclesiasticus says.[1] Do we know the energy for life that is deep within the mystery of our beings, or have we forgotten the strength that resides within us? The Prophecy of Isaiah says, 'Awake, awake, put on your strength.'[2]

The biblical tradition often uses the imagery of the divine arms to refer to God's power and God's love. 'With your strong arm you redeemed your people,' says the Psalmist.[3] God is stronger than the weapons of war, shattering 'the spear' and breaking 'the bow'.[4] In Ezekiel's cloud of 'unknowing' the four living creatures symbolise something of the strength of God's mystery. Like mighty arms the wings of the creatures make 'the sound of many waters' and of 'thunder'. In flight they produce 'the sound of an army', says Ezekiel.[5] And as Mary sings in the Magnificat, 'He has shown strength with his arm . . . He has brought down the powerful from their thrones, and lifted up the lowly.'[6] Yet God is described also as a mother compassionately holding her child to her breast.[7] The imagery ranges from the strength of tremendous power on the one hand to the strength of infinite tenderness on the other.

To be made in the image of God is to say that such strength is at the core of our being. Just as the mystery of our identity is found in the name of God, 'I am who I am', so the strength of our being is derived from the power and the love of God. In the Prophecy of Isaiah, God says to Israel, 'I surname you, even though you do not know me.' Similarly, God says, 'I arm you, even though you do not recognise me.'[8] The more aware we become of our deepest identity the more alert we will be to the strength that is within us. We also, of course, will become more aware of the ways in which we have neglected or abused our strength in the relationships of our lives and in the injustices of the world.

But it is important not to define ourselves primarily in terms of our failures and weaknesses. Our neglect and abuse of strength are not the deepest expressions of who we are. In fact they are false expressions of who we are. We are made in the image of God. Woven into the fabric of our souls is a capacity for true strength. This is not to pretend that failure is not a major mark of the ways in which we try to exercise power or of the ways in which we try to love one another. We get it terribly wrong again and again. Deeper than the failures of our lives, however, is the strength of our inner being. The gift of grace is given to reawaken us to that strength. To be unaware of our strength is not to say that the strength of God's image is not within us. To be unaware is simply to say that we are either underusing our strength or misdirecting it.

One man, in meditating on this theme, saw a defenceless person on the ground being beaten down by another. He felt too weak to help. We often choose not to get involved in the abuses of power that we witness in our lives. In response to the great injustices of our world we often feel powerless. The image speaks also, however, of the way in which dimensions of strength within us are driven down by inner fears and uncertainties. To not believe that we have been endowed with the strength of God's image is to be weakened in our passions for justice and in our determinations to act against wrong. It is also to be radically undermined in our true sense of self.

Julian of Norwich, in her 'Revelations of Divine Love', sees that the throne of God is within her. In the boundless inner kingdom of her soul is the power of God. As Jesus says, 'the kingdom of God is within you',[9] and as the Psalmist says, the throne of God's kingdom 'endures forever'.[10] The capacity for strength planted in the ground of our being has not been uprooted by our failures. We may not be using it for creativity and for justice, or it may have become twisted into a power for wrong and for selfishness, but it is within us waiting to be set free and renewed. The problem is not with power. All power does not corrupt. The problem is what we do, or choose not to do, with the immense resources of strength that reside within us.

The Scriptures refer to God's creative power as the strength that gives birth to the unfolding mystery of the universe. 'By your strength you established the mountains,' writes the Psalmist, 'and the heavens are the work of your hands.'[11] Something of the creative power within the formation of earth's mountains and in the explosive expansion of the cosmos is also within us. It is the strength to bring into being what has never been before, to procreate and to give expression in our lives and relationships to what has never been uttered or envisaged.

As well as being creative, God's power is protective. It

holds back the destructive side of chaos. With a strong sword God will subdue 'the dragon that is in the sea', as the Scriptures say.[12] Having given birth to everything that has being, God passionately opposes the forces that lead to non-being. As the creator and lover of life God hates everything that diminishes and destroys life. Whereas the right hand, the hand of love, gives with unrestrained generosity and abundance, the left hand, the hand of power, defends with law and with protective restraint. God is 'father of orphans', 'protector of widows', and defender of the homeless.[13] The divine power holds back the destructive waters of the sea to lead the oppressed people of Israel into freedom, and breaks the arm of Pharaoh because it has become a false power, wielding the sword of oppression instead of raising the sword of justice.[14]

The capacity for power that has been placed deep within us is given that we too may hold back forces of violence in our world and in our own selves. In the biblical tradition God is the source of all true strength. While the abuse of power is passionately denounced by the prophets, the gift of power itself is celebrated as good because it issues forth from the mystery of God. Just as life cannot be conceived or born without the powerful thrusts of masculine energy and the feminine strength of bearing down in childbirth, so justice will not be done in situations of wrong in our world if we do not allow the energies that God has placed within us to flow forth from our depths. If we shut down to our inner strength and the deep instincts for the protection of life that stir within us we will be as untrue to ourselves as to those who are being wronged in the world.

St Matthew's Gospel provides a picture of Pilate, the powerful Roman governor of Palestine, pretending that he can side-step responsibility for the unjust judgement against

Jesus. 'He took some water', says Matthew, 'and washed his hands before the crowd, saying, "I am innocent of this man's blood."'[15] Does Pilate's action not represent in the extreme what all of us experience in one way or another when we attempt to deny that we carry within ourselves a power for good or for evil? Power, of course, does not refer simply to physical strength or political might but also to intellectual, artistic and financial capacities. Similarly when we reflect on what we are doing with our power, we are not referring only to the individual power that we possess but to the collective might and the corporate capabilities that we are part of. Our membership of society, like our participation in economic and educational communities, carries with it enormous privileges and responsibilities of power.

To know the power for good that is within us and to begin to draw on these energies is to find that our own reawakening to strength can be part of other people's reawakening. One man in meditating on this theme saw himself wearing a golden robe and approaching an ancient temple. Upon entering the temple he was shown a bell rope that had not been used for a long time. He began to pull it with all his might. As the great bell rang other people also began to gather. They too were dressed in golden robes. The meditation speaks of the sacred strength that we have access to. The sounding of the mighty bell that has not been rung for ages is a reclaiming of the strength within us that has been long neglected. The imagery speaks also of the way in which the recovery of strength in one part of our being can awaken dormant strengths in other dimensions of our lives, as well as in other people's lives. We have experienced this and witnessed it from afar when a passion for change in one part of the world can awaken yearnings for freedom and justice among men and women in other parts of the world. We also know, of course, that a surging of destructive energies among one people and in one place can ignite expressions of hatred and violence elsewhere. We are an interwoven web of mutual influences.

To say that love is the greatest of strengths is not to blunt our exercising of true power. The deep desire to use our might for creativity and for justice is part of the image of God within us. If we are serious about opposing evil, it must be with all our strength. Evil's resources are deep. We know this in the struggles of our own lives and see it in the chaos of hatreds in various parts of the world. St John the Divine sees evil emerging out of what appears to be a bottomless pit.[16] Jesus, in confronting the madness of the man whose self-destructive behaviour can be contained by no boundaries, is told that his name is 'Legion'.[17] The forces of evil within us and among us are immeasurable, and so Jesus commissions his disciples to proclaim the gospel with 'power' and with 'authority'.[18] Whether we carry the gospel further into the inner universe of the human spirit or further outwards into the realms of relationship and world concerns, we need powerful and authoritative energies to confront the destructive and deluding forces that threaten life within us and among us.

The prophetic tradition denounces wrong and injustice with a great fire of passion and moral authority. The Prophecy of Amos rebukes the religious for seeing to ritual while neglecting justice: 'I hate, I despise your festivals and take no delight in your solemn assemblies. . . . Instead let justice roll down like waters, and righteousness like an everflowing stream.'[19] The Prophecy of Hosea is furious at the perpetrators of wrong: 'I will fall upon them like a she-bear robbed of her cubs.'[20] Similarly, St Paul says, 'be angry

44

but do not sin'.[21] When we are compassionate about those who suffer we are angry and indignant at the wrongs done to them. Are we in touch with the holy passion for anger that is within us, the strength to be righteously outraged at the wrongs being done in our world?

Jesus taught that we are to love with all our 'strength'.[22] This is what we see him doing in the cleansing of the Jerusalem Temple. Furious that pilgrims are being subjected to exploitative currency exchanges and charged inflated prices to make sacrifice, Jesus explodes with anger at the temple merchants and money changers. 'Making a whip of cords, he drove all of them out of the temple,' says St John. 'He poured out the coins of the money changers and overturned their tables.'[23] In St John's Gospel this is the inauguration of Jesus' ministry in Jerusalem. Similarly, in St Luke's Gospel, Jesus' identification with Isaiah is like a manifesto at the beginning of his ministry in Galilee: 'The Spirit of the Lord is upon me . . . to bring good news to the poor . . . to proclaim release to the captives . . . to let the oppressed go free.'[24] Like the prophets before him he passionately expresses his convictions and his strength.

Despite the clear indications of Jesus' robust action and passion for justice, the religious interpretation of him often has been that of a meek and mild character. These were certainly Edwin Muir's childhood memories from a Bible storybook in his family home. They gave him the impression, he says, 'that Jesus was always slightly ill, a pale invalid with the special gentleness of people who cannot live as others do'.[25] Muir recalls, on the other hand, the opposite impression that was stamped on his memory through childhood encounters with the great workhorses of his family farm in the Orkney Islands. He remembers standing trembling among their legs as they were brought in from the fields, steam rising from their nostrils, sweat staining their hides, and their iron-shod hoofs striking against flagstones in the farmyard. 'I loved and dreaded them,' he writes, 'as an explorer loves and dreads a strange country which he has not yet entered.'[26]

In a poem entitled 'The Horses', Muir later explores this 'strange country' of strength that is within us and between us.[27] The setting of the poem is the still aftermath of what he calls 'the seven days war that put the world to sleep'. The imagery is of nuclear destruction and a terrible misuse of power. Into this desolate world, decimated by a war that is like the antithesis of the seven days of creation, 'the strange horses came . . . like a wild wave charging'. They come from a realm that is far past any place that can be remembered. It is, he says, 'as if they had been sent by an old command' to rediscover a 'long-lost archaic relationship'. They represent a connection with a strength that we have lost contact with. It is, writes Muir, 'as if they had come from their own Eden'. They bring an ancient power for life that has been forgotten. In receiving them and reclaiming the lost relationship, 'life is changed,' he says, 'their coming our beginning'.

How are we to be reconnected to this 'strange country' of strength within ourselves that we have lost sight of? Jesus speaks of faith restoring us to the power that God has placed within us. 'If you have faith the size of a mustard seed,' says Jesus, 'you will say to this mountain, "Move from here to there", and it will move.'[28] The mountain as well as the mustard seed is a metaphor, of course, but Jesus is pointing to the way in which faith releases in our inner being strengths that might have seemed entirely foreign to us, strengths for healing and justice, energies for liberation and love. Where do we find the power to shift the apparently immovable powers of wrong and apathy in our world? Where do we find the strength to let go to love again after we have been betrayed or hurt? 'The kingdom of God is within you', says Jesus. This is not to say that the power that can be released in our lives through faith is *our* power. It is to say, however, that only *we* can release it in ourselves. As Jesus says repeatedly in the Gospel stories of healing and liberation, 'your faith has made you well', 'your faith has saved you'.[29] It is faith that releases the power that God has placed deep within the mystery of our beings, a power that is close to us but from which we have become distant.

A true strength of power does not stand alone. It is wedded to the strength of love, which is also waiting to be rediscovered in our depths. The Jewish mystics liked to speak of power and love being yoked together like oxen ploughing the land. Only when our strength of power is yoked with our strength of love will the fields of our lives truly be cultivated.

This is the combination of strength that we find celebrated in the Scriptures. The creating and redeeming power of the divine are linked inseparably with the strength of love. The One whose creative energies call forth the earth and the heavens, 'the sun to rule the day' and 'the moon and the stars to rule the night', is praised above all else in terms of love, 'for his steadfast love endures forever', says the Psalmist.[30] Similarly, God's redeeming power that frees the oppressed people of Israel and leads them through the wilderness is praised with the same refrain, 'for his steadfast love endures forever'. As the Prophecy of Isaiah says, 'I have made . . . and I will save'.[31] The might of divine creativity that we experience in conception and the might of redemption that we know when new life is born in us out

47

of the failures of our lives are both guided by the strength of love.

Even when the power of God's anger at wrong is heard in the Scriptures, stronger still are the words of love, 'I have loved you with an everlasting love', and 'you will not be forgotten by me'.[32] Greater than the relentless denouncing of sin in the Bible is the assurance that God 'does not deal with us according to our sins'.[33] Love's strength is a boundless flow of mercy. Return therefore to God, says Isaiah, 'for he will abundantly pardon'.[34]

The strength of the divine love is for everything in the whole of creation. 'You love all things that exist', says the Book of Wisdom, 'and detest nothing that you have made.'[35] To be made in the image of God is to be made in the likeness of love. Among the Jewish mystics this leads to a reverencing of the life that is in all things. 'Do not uproot anything that grows unless it is necessary', says the Kabbalah, 'do not kill anything that lives unless it is necessary'.[36] In the Old Testament Scriptures the story is told of how a responsibility for the whole of creation is placed into the hands of Noah,[37] into the hands of humanity's power and humanity's love. The covenant between God and everything that exists, symbolised in the Genesis story by a rainbow that connects heaven and earth, is a promise never to destroy creation. To be made in the image of God is to be part of an eternal promise that has been made to the earth, that our power has been given to us to serve a relationship of love with creation.

Deep in our souls are the promptings of love's strength. When we use the power of force creatively or defensively in our lives and world we are being called at the same time to release from our depths the even greater strength of love. In opposing injustice with all our might we are being called from the very centre of our beings to do so with love. Otherwise, even the goodness of our attempts to fight injustice and inhumanity in the world will become infected by perversions of power.

Jesus is the one who hears the deepest of truths, the call to love. It is a love even for the enemy. Jesus tells the story of the Good Samaritan, who cares for someone from another ethnic group despite the hostilities between their communities. It is a parable of being rereconnected to the strength that is deep within us but which often we have been taught to fear. It is a strength that uncomfortably breaks through the false boundaries of racial and religious differences. Jesus says, 'You have heard that it was said, "You shall love your neighbour and hate your enemy." But I say to you, Love your enemy.'[38]

What does this mean in terms of how we treat our 'enemies'? Rather than using only the power of force against them, we are being called to draw on love's strength as well. This does not mean that we dispense with a true use of power in opposing what is wrong or in defending the oppressed. It does mean, however, that we are to employ, or to deploy, our greatest strength, the strength of love, and to allow love to guide our use of power.

This is a strength that we have been given not simply for those who are part of our nation or our class or race. This is a strength that we have been given for all people and for the whole of creation. Jesus does not teach a solidarity that limits love to the boundaries of one particular group. 'If you love those who love you,' says Jesus, 'what credit is that to you? For even sinners love those who love them.'[39] Jesus sides with the poor and the oppressed. This is very clear from the Gospel texts. His anger at injustice, however, does not lead him to abandon the rich and the powerful.

The Gospels abound in examples of Jesus having meals and conversations with members of the oppressing classes and religious elite of his country. Love does not replace one group solidarity with another. Rather, it breaks through all attempts to confine the generosity of God. 'Love your enemies', says Jesus, 'so that you may be children of your Father in heaven, for he makes his sun rise on the evil and on the good, and sends rain on the righteous and on the unrighteous.'[40] Jesus shows us that deep in the gift of our being is the gift of love. At the heart of the image of God in us is the mystery of self-giving. It is to these depths that we are being recalled.

A Scottish monk from a little religious community outside Edinburgh used to tell the story of the beginnings of his community. The three founding members went on retreat together to a neighbouring monastery. There they were guided by a wise old monk. On the first day of the retreat the old monk shuffled into the room, sat down and said, 'Now there is just one thing that I am going to tell you today. God loves you. Go away and ponder this.' So they spent the first day reflecting on the mystery that God is love. On the second day the old man again shuffled into the room, sat down and said, 'Now there is just one thing that I am going to tell you today. You can love God. Go away and ponder this truth.' So they spent the second day reflecting on the mystery that not only does God desire us but that deep in our inner beings we have a desire and a capacity to love God. They began to wonder what on earth the old monk could possibly say on the third day. Was the relationship of God loving us and us loving God not a complete expression of the gospel mystery? On the third day when the old monk came in and sat down, he said, 'There is just one thing that I am going to tell you before you leave. You can love one another. Now go away and live this mystery together as a community.' We are called to live from our deepest strength, the strength to love. Jesus says to his disciples, 'This is my commandment, that you love one another as I have loved you.'[41]

Part of true strength, of course, is a love for oneself. As the Scriptures say, 'love your neighbour as yourself'.[42] We are called to die to the falseness of what we have become in our lives, to hate what is untrue in ourselves. But unless we love our true selves, formed by God in our mother's womb, the love that we try to offer others will be infected by the same doubts and lack of reverence that we have for ourselves.

A ninth-century Indian mystic once dreamt that he met God. In the dream God asked him what he desired. The Indian answered, 'I desire what you desire, O God', to which God replied, 'It is you I desire'.[43] Too often in our religious traditions we have been given the impression that, although God loves us, it would be dangerous to do the same ourselves.

The ninth-century Irish teacher, Eriugena, says that there is nothing that has been created by Love that does not desire love.[44] This challenges us to see that in every person there is a deep desire for love, even though that desire may have been lost sight of. It challenges us to see also that our enemy is someone who at an essential level longs for reconciliation, even though that longing may lie buried deep within. Similarly, it challenges those of us who work for justice and peace to see that we are not the only ones who yearn for what is right. The challenge is to be awakened to the yearnings that lie hidden in the human soul. These are the yearnings of love that God has planted within us. We become tortured human beings when we deny the desire for love.

The mystery of love has been woven into the very heart of all things. William Blake speaks of the 'fibres of love' that hold together the whole tissue of life.[45] 'Love one another', says Jesus.[46] This is the truth that has been carved into the human heart despite our betrayal of it. 'Be servants of one another in love', says St Paul.[47] This is the law that has been etched into our beings even though we ignore it. But why do we ignore it? Why do we neglect the summons that issues up from the very ground of life? Is it not because, if we obey the truth, our ego must die? 'If any want to become my followers,' says Jesus, 'let them deny themselves and take up their cross and follow me.'[48]

Although true power and true love are yoked inseparably together, there has been the tendency to divide them in thought as well as in practice. The exercise of great power is deemed to be incompatible with great love. It is thought that to achieve power we must be ruthless. Love, on the other hand, is often identified with a resignation of power. It is assumed that to be loving is to be uninterested in power. But the conflict is not between the strength of love and the strength of power. Both belong to the image of God at the heart of our being. Rather, the conflict is between the strength of love and the strength of false power, between the giving of ourselves and a fearful withholding of ourselves.

One person, in meditating on the relationship between power and love saw an image of God giving birth. God's hands were helping the child into the world. The newborn was held first in God's left hand, then in her right hand, before being placed into the arms of the person who was meditating. This is an image of life coming forth from the mystery of God, and of all things coming to us through the power of God as well as through the love of God. It is an image also of the sacredness of life being shared, of the placing of ourselves into one another's hands.

To know that power and love belong inseparably together in the mystery of God, and therefore that they are inseparably interwoven in the mystery of our own being, is to call for a radically new way of understanding greatness. As Jesus says to his disciples, 'You know that the rulers of the Gentiles lord it over them, and their great ones are tyrants over them. It will not be so among you; but whoever wishes to be great among you must be your servant.'[49]

Love and power are both emanations of the mystery of God's strength, and they both flow from the depths of our being, made as we are in the image of God. If, however, the power that is in us and at our disposal is not held in relationship with love then our capacity for power becomes instead a capacity for evil. Power can dazzle us and blind us with its immensity and allure. Unless it is guided by love it becomes a source of wrong in our relationships and in our world. This is not to say that our heart is essentially evil or that we are always predisposed towards abusing power. Our strength of power, however, tends towards wrongdoing when it is not being guided by the greater strength of love. There is the tendency in us to try to make towers of Babel for ourselves, 'to make a name for ourselves' as Genesis says.[50] But we do this only when we have lost confidence in the true strength that is within us. It is this temptation that Jesus resists when Satan tries to lure him with the false power of 'all the kingdoms of the world and their splendour'. Jesus says, 'Away with you, Satan!'[51]

The Old Testament prophets often point to the corruption of power when it is not guided by mercy and love. Ezekiel says that the shepherds of the house of Israel have abused the gift of power. They have become harsh in their treatment of the flock. Instead of feeding the people they are serving themselves. Instead of containing the nation with security they are scattering the people and fragmenting the nation.[52]

The strength of love is to be like a bridle placed over the strength of power. This is not to suppress the powerful urges that are within us. Wholeness cannot be achieved through trying to hold them down. Rather, the great surges of strength in us must be seized by love. They need constantly to be pulled in the direction of new life by the strength of love. Love is a guiding energy. It leads us not simply to refrain from wrongdoing but into an active doing of good. As the Prophecy of Isaiah says, 'cease to do evil, learn to do good'.[53]

The early Celtic teacher Pelagius makes the point that love does not just restrain us from stealing, for instance. Much more importantly it inspires us to share our possessions. 'I do not wish you to suppose that righteousness consists simply in not doing evil, since not to do good is also evil', he says. 'Indeed, you are instructed . . . not only not to take bread away from one who has it but willingly to bestow your own on one who has none.'[54] Pelagius indicates that the person who is rich and refuses to share food with the hungry may be causing more deaths than a terrible murderer. Jesus' judgement parable in Matthew 25 is a story of condemnation not against those who actively have broken the law but against those who passively have done nothing about sharing themselves and their resources. On the last day, says St Matthew's Gospel, the Son of Man will declare, 'I was hungry and you gave me no food, I was thirsty and you gave me nothing to drink, I was a stranger and you did not welcome me'.[55]

The gift of power is given to serve love and to safeguard

life, not to limit it and restrict it. This is true also of religious power, including the teachings and moral strictures of religion. Jesus was opposed not to the law of Judaism but to the way the law was being used, as a burden to the people instead of as a servant to them. 'Do not think that I have come to abolish the law or the prophets,' says Jesus. 'I have come not to abolish but to fulfil.'[56] The religious leaders were using the law of Sabbath observance against the people instead of for them. It was meant to release them from work on one day of the week so that they could rest. It was not intended to prevent them from eating or from doing good on that day. Jesus was not wanting to do away with the law but to dethrone it, so that it would become the servant of love rather than love's master. He criticises the religious authorities of his day not because of what they teach but because of what they do. 'You tithe mint, dill, and cumin', he says to them, but 'have neglected the weightier matters of the law: justice and mercy and faith. It is these you ought to have practised without neglecting the others.'[57] The true power of religious observance is given to make way for the strength of love.

William Blake ridicules religion's tendency to focus more on what we are *not* to do than on what we *are* to do, and on highlighting restraint rather than freedom. St Paul says, 'For freedom Christ has set us free. Stand fast, therefore, and do not submit again to a yoke of slavery.'[58] Yet so much of our religious practice is governed by a fear of freedom rather than a confidence in it. In his poem 'The Garden of Love', Blake describes entering a beautiful garden with a chapel in it, only to find a sign 'Thou shalt not' written above the chapel doorway. 'And Priests in black gowns were walking their rounds', he writes, 'and binding with briars my joys & desires.'[59] Religion, he says, ends up cursing our desires instead of blessing them, suppressing our longings instead of liberating them, forgetting that it is God who has planted within us our yearnings for love and joy. We become like Muir's childhood impression of Jesus, 'a pale invalid'. The deep strengths of our humanity are sapped of energy instead of being nourished.

The sacred emanations of God's being are all one. They flow forth from the same source and belong to one another. In the mystery of our beings, the emanations of God's image are like a single flow of light. If one is obscured the others also will be hidden. If we are not guided by love in our lives our wisdom also will be dimmed. From various perspectives the emanations may seem different, like light passing through different colours of glass, but they all flow from the same mystery of light.

Each emanation is given to be in harmony with the others. Power on its own can give the impression that might is right, and that the world is simply at our disposal to do with as we choose. On the other hand, when the gift of power in us flows together with love, or with wisdom and mystery, then we know more clearly the limits of power. When we are alert to the mystery of creation we are less likely to use our power abusively in relation to creation. When we perceive the wisdom that is in other human beings we are less prone to treat them as objects for our own purposes. The abuse of power distorts the whole of the divine image in us. If power is allowed to dominate, mystery is trampled, wisdom becomes a pawn, and love is exploited.

How are we to be recalled to a true vitality of strength in our lives? The Scriptures say that we are to seek God's strength.[60] But this is not a strength that is foreign to us. It is the strength at the very heart of our beings, but from which we have become separated. As we have already noted in relation to the other emanations, we need to establish disciplines of stillness and awareness in our lives if we are to hear the true depths of who we are. Otherwise we forget the true characteristics of strength and allow distorted images of power and love to dominate our lives and relationships. As the Prophecy of Isaiah says, 'those who wait for the Lord shall renew their strength'. [61] In an attentiveness to our inner beings the strength that is in us can be rediscovered and released.

But even if we establish practices of stillness and contemplation, how are we to know what true strength is? How can we be freed from our self-deceiving notions of power and love? In the Christian tradition Christ is the perfect expression of love. He is also, as St Paul says, 'the power of God'.[62] Christ embodies the mystery of God's strength, showing us the power and the love that have been planted at the heart of our beings. But just as Christ 'the wisdom of God' can seem like foolishness to the world because it is a childlike wisdom, so Christ 'the power of God' can seem like weakness to the world because it is a self-limiting power.

Early in the Church's history Christ is identified with the suffering servant of the Old Testament, a figure of no outward majesty or show of power. And yet the suffering servant, says Isaiah, is the one to whom 'the arm of the Lord has been revealed'.[63] He is among the truly strong and the truly great, not because of any visible might and prestige, but 'because he poured out himself to death', says Isaiah.[64] Ultimate strength is the strength of self-giving.

This is what Jesus had taught his disciples, 'to lay down one's life for one's friends', as he had put it.[65] When towards the end of his ministry he warns the disciples that he will suffer at the hands of the religious leadership in

Jerusalem, Peter rebukes him and says, 'This must never happen to you'. Jesus replies, 'Get behind me, Satan! You are a stumbling block to me.'[66] Peter's words represent a belief in false strength, not a pouring out of oneself in love but a preserving of oneself in fear. This is not to deny that in the Gospel accounts Jesus is frightened by the powers of darkness that begin to envelop him. In St Luke's Gospel he is described as sweating drops of blood in the Garden of Gethsemane as he faces the forces of death.[67] In the midst of his fear an angel of strength appears to him, but it is not a strength that leads him away from the fearful confronta-tion with death. Rather, it is a strength that enables him to pour himself out in love as he approaches death. This is the strength that is pointed to after the crucifixion in the words of the risen Christ. 'Look at my hands and my feet', he says.[68] They bear the marks of suffering. They are the true marks of the strength of love.

To follow the way of Christ is to be restored to the strength that God has woven into the depths of our being. It is what Blake calls the 'Mysterious Offering of Self for Another'.[69] We find it deep in the human spirit and have witnessed it at the costliest moments of life when there is self-giving love and a pouring out of what is most precious for another. We have experienced it in our relationships when we are loved unconditionally and forgiven for dis-loyalties and wrongs committed. 'The Forgiveness of Sins', says Blake, is what will truly 'Humanize' us.[70] To experi-ence the grace of forgiveness is to be called back to our true selves. It is to see the falseness of what we have become and to turn from our failures. Jesus offers this grace even to those who have wronged him most. From the cross he prays for them, 'Father, forgive them for they do not know what they are doing.'[71]

The Strength of the Self

Where is our strength? It is not in clinging to life and to all that we might claim as ours. Rather, it is in letting go to life, both in our living and in our dying. It is in letting go to love. Jesus points to the deepest place of strength when he prays from the cross, 'Father, into your hands I commend my spirit'.[72] These are Jesus' final words, but even more than being his words of death they are his words of life. They speak of where his strength has always been found, in the power and love of God at the heart of his being. It is into these depths that he allows himself to fall. As the Scriptures say, 'underneath are the everlasting arms'.[73] Deeper than death is the strength of God. To let go to these depths is to be set free from any power that might threaten us.

One of the most frequently repeated phrases in the Scriptures is 'do not fear'. It has been said that it is repeated 365 times, once for every day of the year! The Prophecy of Isaiah says, 'Do not fear, for I am with you, do not be afraid, for I am your God; I will strengthen you, I will help you, I will uphold you with my victorious right hand.'[74] Deeper than any fear in us is the eternally strong foundation of our beings, the strength of God within us.

Words for Meditation

'You endowed me with strength like your own' *(Ecclesiasticus 17:3).*

59

4

THE BEAUTY OF THE SELF

The heart at the centre of the human body represents the beauty that is at the heart of life. We often define ourselves in terms of the ugliness of what we have done or become rather than in terms of the essence of our life. We are made in the image of God, in the image of the One who is Beauty.

Think of a beautiful plant suffering from blight. If botanists were shown such a plant, even if they had never seen that particular type of plant before, they would define it in terms of its essential features and life-force. They would not define it in terms of its blight. Rather, the blight would be described as foreign to the plant, as attacking its essence. This may seem an obvious point botanically, but perhaps it is such an obvious point that we have missed the point when it comes to defining what is deepest within us. In our Western Christian tradition we have tended to understand human nature in terms of its blight. The doctrine of original sin defines us as essentially sinful rather than seeing that sin is attacking the essence of our being. What is deepest in us is the beauty of our origins.

The Scriptures refer to God as the King of beauty.[1] Our origins are in God. We are sons and daughters of beauty, or as the Celtic tradition of fairy tale imagines, we are princes and princesses of beauty. The power of fairy tale is its ability to name dimensions of the depths of our being that we have forgotten and need to recover. One of George MacDonald's nineteenth-century fairy tales is the story of a prince who at birth is separated from his noble mother by a wicked witch.[2] He grows up not knowing who he is and is forced to live only in the day. He knows nothing of the night's darkness. Only as a young man does he finally experience the mystery of the night. Only through the night's way of seeing does he finally discover that he is the son of the beautiful Lady Aurora. This is a story of the need to rediscover our inner sight and to uncover our truest, but hidden, identity.

In the biblical tradition our deepest place of identity is the beauty of Eden. The Genesis picture is not of the garden being destroyed but rather of Adam and Eve moving into a type of exile from it. Eden, of course, is not a place from which we are distant in space and time. Rather, it is a dimension within ourselves from which we have become separated. Like Adam and Eve we have become fugitives from the beauty of our origins.

Edwin Muir explores this theme in his poem 'One Foot in Eden'. He describes our beauty as distorted. It has been covered over and blighted by wrongdoing and sin, he says, 'yet still from Eden springs the root as clean as on the starting day'.[3] Our rootedness in Eden has not been undone. Our essence partakes of a beauty that is deeper than any ugliness in our lives.

The Prophecy of Ezekiel says that to be born of Eden is to be 'perfect in beauty'.[4] This is not to be naive about the distortions and ugliness in us, whether individually or collectively. It is to say, however, that our deepest identity is in beauty and not in ugliness. The Jewish tradition has consistently held together the belief that life is essentially beautiful with the recognition that it is distorted by evil. This is to hold on to the foundational truth of the biblical tradition, that despite every failing in our lives the roots of our being remain in the goodness of God. A prayer that is used by millions of Jews around the world each day includes the words, 'My God, the soul you placed within me is pure. You created it, You fashioned it, You breathed it into me. You preserve and safeguard it within me.'[5] The essence of who we are has not been erased by sin but covered over by sin.

We find this theme of essential beauty in the Hebrew love song, Song of Songs. God, as the Lover of our ever-living souls, says, 'How beautiful you are, my love, how very beautiful! . . . You are altogether beautiful, my love; there is no flaw in you.'[6] Of course there are flaws in us. We know that, sometimes to the point of almost entirely defining ourselves in terms of our flaws. But do we know that deeper still is our root in beauty? Do we know that the centre of our being is beautiful, made as we are in the image of God? Redemption is about being reconnected to the beauty that has been planted at the heart of all being.

Jesus says, 'The kingdom of heaven is like treasure hidden in a field.'[7] Once we have discovered the treasure, he says, we should let go of everything else and buy the field. So it is when we discover the treasure of beauty that is hidden at the heart of life. We need to let go of other preconceptions of what life is and invest totally in what Edwin Muir calls this 'treasure trove'.[8] It is inexhaustibly deep and rich.

The Old Testament points to the Temple as the place of 'excellence and beauty'.[9] It is the place where God dwells. King Solomon receives the divine assurance that God's 'heart shall forever be there'.[10] The Temple was regarded as the centre of the holy city, and at the heart of the Temple was the Holy of Holies, the Temple's inner sanctum. It was a sign of God's presence and a symbol of the inner reality of the temple of our beings. As St Paul says, 'Do you not know that you are God's temple?'[11] Similarly, St Peter speaks of the beauty of the 'inner self', the holy of holies at the heart of our being.[12]

Whether we speak of the temple of creation as the Celtic tradition does, and the beauty of earth, sea and sky, or the Jerusalem Temple, and the sacredness of any religious site, these are outward signs of an inner reality. They are pointing to the temple 'not made with hands', as the Scriptures say, the eternal place of God's dwelling.[13] William Blake calls this the 'Jerusalem in every Man'.[14] The outward grandeur of the temple of creation, like the beauty and harmony of a great cathedral, are signs of the everlasting inner beauty of the soul.

Jesus says, 'The kingdom of God is within you.'[15] It is an eternal kingdom, unbounded by space and time. As the fourteenth-century English mystic Julian of Norwich sees in one of her 'Revelations of Divine Love', 'I saw the soul as wide as if it were an infinite world, and as if it were a blessed kingdom.'[16] Or as Symeon the New Theologian says, 'I who am mortal and an insignificant person in the world, behold the entire Creator of the world in myself.' There, he says, 'I embrace all blossoming life'.[17] It is not away from our depths that we are to look for beauty but to the heart of every living thing.

Beauty, as we have seen, is a favourite theme with Edwin Muir. In his poem, 'The Brothers', he imagines, as in a dream, his two brothers who had died fifty years before, or what he calls 'twenty thousand days ago'.[18] He sees them in the beauty of their boyhood playing innocently in a field. A brilliant light streams from their faces. They were 'like two revolving suns', he says. 'A brightness poured from head to head, so strong I could not see their eyes or look into their paradise.' Then Muir asks, 'How could I be so dull, twenty thousand days ago, not to see they were beautiful?' The poem raises the same question in each of us. We will have memories of missing the moment in our lives, when instead of seeing the beauty in those whom we love we have focused on their flaws. How could we be so dull not to have seen the beauty that is within them?

Muir's vision of his brothers' beauty is a fleeting one, for 'the dream was soon away', he writes. Instead of the brightness that had poured forth from them, 'a darkness covered every head. Frowns twisted the original face, and through that mask we could not see the beauty and the buried grace.' The original face is beautiful, but it becomes covered by masks of ugliness, by fear and selfishness, by envy and greed. To the extent that we collude with these inclinations, or to the extent that we become conscious of such ugliness in us, we experience shame. As the prophet Isaiah says, 'instead of beauty shame'.[19]

In his autobiography, Muir describes the move in his adolescence from the Orkney Islands to the highly industrialised city of Glasgow. It has the effect of distancing him from beauty:

I walked to and from my work each day through a slum. . . . These journeys filled me with a sense of degradation: the crumbling houses, the twisted faces, the obscene words casually heard in passing, the ancient, haunting stench of pollution and decay, the arrogant women, the mean men, the terrible children, daunted me, and at last filled me with an immense, blind dejection. I had seen only ordinary people before; but on some of the faces that I passed every day now there seemed to be things written which only a fantastic imagination could have created, and I shrank from reading them and quickly learned not to see. After a while . . . I got used to these things; I walked through the slums as if they were an ordinary road leading from my home to my work.[20]

The account describes a loss in Muir that parallels his earlier loss of innocent wisdom in boyhood. Now, however, it is a loss of the sense of life's beauty. It marks a transition in which he comes to see the 'natural' as ugly. And yet ugliness, as he perceives later in his life, is in fact unnatural. It is our beauty that is most truly natural for it issues up from our place of deepest origin. Our departure from beauty, or our exile from what is at the heart of life, is what leads us into all sorts of unnaturalness.

Once we have lost true naturalness in our lives it is difficult to recover it. As Muir writes in his autobiography, 'naturalness does not come easily to the awkward human race'.[21] This is Muir's way of pointing to our need for grace, but it is not a grace that is opposed to what is truly natural. Rather, it is a grace that restores us to what is truly natural, including the beauty that is deep within the human countenance.

In the Celtic tradition, John Scotus Eriugena uses the analogy of sin being like an infection of the soul. Just as leprosy has the power to distort the human face and make it appear ugly and even monstrous, so sin has the power to distort the countenance of the soul. So distorted does our inner being become that it begins to appear essentially ugly. We come to believe that it is naturally grotesque. But the beauty of the soul is deeper than any ugliness in us. The role of grace, says Eriugena, is not to give us a different inner countenance but to restore us to our true inner countenance. The lepers in St Luke's Gospel who are healed by Jesus are not given new faces. Rather, they are restored to their true faces, to their original identities. Similarly grace releases in us the beauty of our genesis. We are restored to our true selves.

Eriugena and Muir both point to the distorting power of evil. The Scriptures refer to the destructive dragon of the sea, Leviathan, as 'the twisting serpent'.[22] St John the Divine describes 'the ancient serpent' as 'the deceiver of the whole world'.[23] The imagery is of a power that misrepresents what is true and perverts what is beautiful. Similarly, William Blake speaks of the shadow in us, or what he calls the 'Spectre'.[24] It rages against our true nature and against our beauty. For Blake, of course, the twisting power of the 'Spectre' includes much religious belief and practice. Again and again religion has been fearful of what is deepest in us and has raged against our most natural desires as if they were essentially monstrous.

While the Old Testament speaks of the beauty of the Temple, it bears witness also to the defiling of beauty. 'Your foes have roared within your holy place', says the Psalmist.[25] They have 'desecrated' her beauty and she is 'no longer free'.[26] The words point to the way in which sin, as well as defiling our beauty, also leads to a type of imprisonment or bondage. It is a bondage to what is unnatural.

During my years in Portsmouth, a city with very little open natural space, I was particularly aware of bird life. Especially there was a pair of collar doves in the garden who often would wake me up in the early hours cooing at the top of our chimney pot. On one occasion as I sat writing at my desk, I became aware of a sound of great

The Beauty of the Self

struggle in the study chimney. The sound came closer and closer. Eventually I realised it was a bird of considerable size stuck in the flue. For many years the fireplace had been sealed up at ground level. I was busy and did not relish the thought of having to unblock the chimney. Even less appealing was the idea of a big bird flying around in my study.

I began to pull down into the fireplace the old pieces of newspaper that had been used to block it off. Decades of chimney dirt crumbled down with the paper. I was covered with soot and there were all sorts of uncertainties in me about how I was going to handle the bird. Eventually I saw her tail feathers and realised it was a collar dove. When I laid hold of her she immediately became still. Her feathers were filthy and she was frightened. I carried her into the garden and placed her on a wall, well away from the family dog! The bird sat totally still in a state of shock. I went back to the study to get on with my work, and when I returned half an hour later she was still sitting on the wall covered in soot. This time, however, as I approached she flew and as she flew the soot fell off. In mid-air in the afternoon sunshine she was an image of freedom and beauty.

For many days afterwards the experience of the bird's struggle and release was with me. It was as if she represented something in me that had been trapped and was needing to be set free. It was especially the sight of her sitting on the wall stunned that haunted me. In one sense she had been free at that point, but in another sense she was not free until she flew with her beauty. Sometimes in the early morning when the collar doves wake me up with their cooing I remember. There is a beauty in us that is needing to be aroused. William Blake describes us as a 'Sleeping

67

Humanity'. He says, 'Awake! awake O sleeper of the land of shadows, wake! expand!'[27] His words speak of being released from within ourselves and flying freely in our beauty.

In the early 1990s I spent time with the English Benedictine monk Bede Griffiths at his Indian ashram in Tamil Nadu. One of the themes that characterises much of his teaching is also the title of one of his works, *Return to the Centre*.[28] He speaks of the way in which we have become distant from ourselves and thus from God at the heart of our being. The return to God is the return to the centre of all life. Bede died in the mid-1990s but he occasionally visits me in my dream life. In one dream he said very simply to me, 'Keep on reading Sleeping Beauty. Keep on reading Sleeping Beauty.' We need to read the deepest text of who we are, listening for the intimations of beauty that issue up from the heart of our being. It is the Beauty that is at the heart of all being.

The Celtic tradition uses the image of listening for the heartbeat of God.[29] It is derived from the Gospel account of John the Beloved leaning against Jesus at the last supper. The legend is that John thus heard the heartbeat of God. He became an image of listening within all things for the One who is the very beat of life. It is the beat of Beauty without which nothing that is would be.

Similarly we can be alert in the inner landscape of our souls to the intimations of promise that are uttered by God from the heart of our being. It was there that Isaiah heard the words of assurance, 'you are precious in my sight . . . and I love you'.[30] Such words are like an inner correspondence to the outward signs of promise that are offered throughout the biblical tradition. For Noah it is a rainbow of promise that speaks of 'the everlasting covenant between

God and every living creature on the earth'.[31] It is a promise that the beauty at the heart of life will not be destroyed.

We all have received intimations of promise through the mystery of creation, in light breaking through clouds, in the return of geese in the spring, in the emergence of brilliant flowers and colourful fruit from the darkness of the ground. One of my experiences of promise came to me at the north end of the holy island of Iona on a beach called the White Strand of the Monks. It was there in the ninth century that the Abbot of Iona had been martyred at the hands of Norse invaders. It is a beach of beauty and of pain. Many have sought it out as a place of solitude and prayer. The promise that I experienced came as I stood with my wife on the strand. I was full of doubt. I felt a failure and could see in my own life and in the life of the community to which I belonged little more than ugliness. As we looked out towards the Island of Storm to the north of the strand, a rainbow formed around us. We found ourselves standing in its arch, its pillars planted firmly on either side of us.

That experience of promise was given years ago. I am still interpreting it, and I suppose will never exhaust its meaning, but I knew that we had been addressed by a Beauty deeper than ugliness and a Strength greater than failure. It is to such experiences of promise that the prophets point when they hear within themselves words of deep assurance. 'What is desolate in you I will replant', says the Prophecy of Ezekiel, and your soul again will be 'like the garden of Eden'.[32]

The beauty of God that is deep within the mystery of our being will not be rediscovered simply through thinking about it or talking about it. Rather, we will be changed by

69

experiencing beauty and by allowing ourselves to touch it and to be touched by it. Edwin Muir recounts a transformative dream in which beauty is reawakened in him. The setting of the dream is a place that he associated with an innocence of beauty, the family farm on the island of Wyre in the Orkneys where he had spent his early childhood:

> I came to a little chapel or shrine on the shore. On one wall a brown clay image was hanging: a weatherbeaten image of an old woman naked to the waist, with sun-burned, wrinkled dugs. I went up to the image, and as if I were fulfilling some ritual pressed one of the nipples with my finger. A trembling flowed over the figure, and, like a wave running across another in counter-motion, the texture changed; the clay quivered and rippled with life, all the marks of age vanishing in that transparent flood; the breast shone smooth and round, and rose and fell with living breath. At the same time in the centre of my breast I felt a hot, tingling fire, and I knew that a yellow sun was blazing there, and with its beams, which filled my body with light and soft power, was raising the image from the dead. The figure came down from the wall, a dark brown girl, and stood beside me. That is all I remember about the dream, which ended before I reached the Bu [the family farm], though I felt a great longing to return there. It was as if the dream, having set out to take me back to that house which I loved so much, were offering me something else instead, reanimating another image of whose existence I did not know.[33]

It is in touching the heart or the breast, the place of beauty, that a new consciousness is awakened in Muir. It is a beauty that has been raised, he says, as if 'from the dead'.

He experiences it as something that has been lost sight of in himself but also in his relationships and collectively in his wider community and world. Later Muir was to write that in coming into touch with the beauty that is at the heart of life, it was, he said, as if I had 'struck up a first acquaintance with myself'.[34]

We need to become acquainted, perhaps for the first time, with this inner sanctuary of beauty. As William Blake says, we must 'learn to adore' the depths that are within us, what he calls 'the buried Soul & all its Gems'.[35] We can spend our whole lives searching everywhere else for this treasure and fail to see that it is closer to us than we are to ourselves. Symeon the New Theologian describes how for years he 'laboriously sought' Christ as distant from himself, when 'I suddenly came to know that he was in myself; and in the center of my heart he appeared like the light of a sun, round as a circle'.[36] The Prophecy of Ezekiel speaks of coming to know the 'exits' and 'entrances' of the temple.[37] Just as we learn how to enter sacred sites of prayer and beauty, so we may learn to enter the inner temple of beauty within ourselves in order to be renewed in our depths.

But how are we to know of this inner sanctuary if we have become separated from it? Christ, as we have seen, describes his ministry in terms of coming to bear witness to the truth. He comes to reveal what has been planted in the very depths of our human nature. As Eriugena says, Christ is 'the art of the almighty Artist'.[38] He is the perfect expression of God. The beauty that we see in Christ is not a beauty that is foreign to us, although it may be a beauty from which we have become foreign. To glimpse the truth of the beauty that has been woven into the essence of our souls is to begin to be set free. 'You shall know the truth,' says Jesus, 'and the truth shall set you free.'[39] It is a truth that frees us from the ugliness that we feared to be deepest in ourselves.

St John describes Jesus as 'close to the Father's heart'.[40] He comes to make known God's heart to us, and thus our own heart, for we are made in the image of God. He comes to cleanse the temple of our beings, just as outwardly he cleansed the Jerusalem Temple.[41] As Pelagius says, Christ comes with grace to wash us so that we may 'become more beautiful day by day'.[42] This is no superficial cleansing but a deep renewing of inner beauty. Just as Jesus says that it is what comes out of a man that defiles him,[43] so it is what comes out of a person that makes him or her truly beautiful. 'Woe to you, scribes and Pharisees, hypocrites!', says Jesus. 'For you clean the outside of the cup and of the plate, but inside you are full of greed and self-indulgence. You blind Pharisee! First clean the inside of the cup, so that the outside also may become clean.'[44]

The grace of repentance, which is a turning around within ourselves, is given that we may turn again to the root of our beauty, to the Soul of all souls who is the heart of beauty. Part of repentance is to face the ugliness of what we have done and become, but we are not to get stuck there and become obsessive about our ugliness. The journey of repentance is about moving deeper than ugliness to the beauty that is at the heart of our being. The journey, however, does not take us around our failures but through them. We need to confront the twisted disfigurements of what we have become in our lives and relationships. William Blake speaks of 'the spiritual sword that lays open the hidden heart'.[45] 'Sharper than any two-edged sword', says the writer to the Hebrews, we are pierced by truth.[46] It severs the distortions in us from the heart of our being. It cuts us open to reveal the beauty that is deeper still.

This of course is a painful journey as infections are cut out of us. It can also be a frightening journey, for although there is an infinity of colour in our heart it may have become so dark that we no longer see its brightness. One woman in meditating on this theme saw that, although her heart was like an ancient sanctuary with wonderfully massive granite pillars, it was dark at the centre and she was afraid to enter. Blake describes entering the darkness of our inner sanctuary with a 'globe of fire', there to search out 'caves of solitude & dark despair' and all sorts of degradation.[47] But as a twelfth-century Indian mystic says, the true seeker is undeterred in entering the depths of the self in order to find the treasure of beauty: 'In his desire to know it, he will not retreat before the dragons who devour souls.'[48] Although the inner sanctuary of our souls can seem frightening and strange, it also has an ancient familiarity about it that reassures us in our searching. As we repent of the uglinesses that have come to characterise our lives, beautiful shafts of light emerge in the darkness of our inner sanctuary.

The recovery of beauty within us is not simply a return to our natural depths. Nature, as we have noted, is a gift of God, but it is now deeply marred. Therefore, the resurrection of our beauty, as Eriugena says, is a combination of 'nature and grace'.[49] While nature is the gift of being, in which beauty has been planted deep within us, grace is the gift of wellbeing, in which the woundedness of our beauty is healed. Using an ancient system of numerology, which appears in much Celtic artwork, Eriugena says that nature is represented by the number 5. This also is the number of Christ's wounds. The number 5, therefore, refers to the woundedness of nature. Grace, on the other hand, is represented by the number 3. This is the number of the Holy

Trinity. Therefore, 5 plus 3, or nature plus grace, equals 8, which is the number of resurrection. Christ's resurrection occurs on the eighth day or the day after the seventh day. The Celtic tradition thus points to redemption as a marriage of nature and grace. The redemption of our beauty is not simply a looking to the gift of nature. But neither is it simply a looking to the gift of grace. Grace is given to restore us to the beauty of our God-given nature.

The beauty that is within all things is an expression of the mystery of God. It reveals something of the One whom the Book of Wisdom calls the 'Author of beauty'.[50] It also reveals something of the mystery of our being, made as we are in the image of God. Yet we often treat the manifestations of beauty merely as objects rather than as icons. Instead of seeing them as windows into the depths of the mystery we view them only at their surface.

The Prophecy of Ezekiel speaks of our tendency to 'prostitute' beauty, to think that we can possess it and exploit it as a commodity.[51] This is what has happened in much of our Western culture. Expressions of beauty are turned into objects to be owned and sold, including the beauty of creation and the beauty of the human body. Instead of being regarded as a spiritual document in which we may read eternal truths, the human body is treated as a commodity of flesh and energy. This is as true in much of our corporate management of people and organising of labour as it is of our advertising techniques and sex industries.

Many modern artists reflect on this sense of degradation in their portrayals of the human body as twisted and fragmented. Late in the nineteenth century the French artist Auguste Rodin began to prefigure in his sculpture the modern world's perception and treatment of the human form. His 'Iris: Messenger of the Gods' (1890) depicts a woman in a frenzy of movement, distorted and off balance. The figure is lacking part of its head as well as one of its arms and its vagina is open to public view. 'Iris' prophetically announces the lack of mystery, the distortion of power and the exploiting of sexual energy that have become dominating characteristics of the Western world. The human body is viewed as object rather than as mystery.

There are, of course, fine exceptions to this general pattern in relation to the human body. There is a great yearning today throughout the Western world for a re-integration of body and spirit, of creation and spirituality. Our biblical tradition offers us foundations for the recovery of this integration. The human form is viewed as made in the image of God and as temple of the Spirit. The Scriptures also call our attention to the terrible abuses and distortions of the beauty of the body. A central theme in the prophetic tradition and in the New Testament is the suffering servant, 'so marred was his appearance, beyond human semblance', says Isaiah.[52] It is an image of painful disfigurement:

He had no form or majesty that we should look at him,
nothing in his appearance that we should desire him.
He was despised and rejected by others;
a man of suffering and acquainted with infirmity;
and as one from whom others hide their faces
he was despised, and we held him of no account.[53]

The Scriptures do not naively celebrate the beauty and the holiness of the human body. They call us to be aware of what has gone wrong, and of the need for justice and healing. Again and again they point to those who suffer from the disfiguring powers of disease and hunger, people's lives twisted by poverty and injustice, the beauty of women abused by men. There is the haunting image of the concubine from Bethlehem gang-raped and tortured through a long night.[54] There is the story of King David so confused by his longings for the beauty of Bathsheba that he is driven to the madness of arranging her husband's death.[55] These images and stories speak of what we know and witness in our world and in our lives today.

In the Christian tradition Jesus is identified as the Suffering Servant. He represents not only the beauty that is within us but the pain and disfigurement that characterise our lives and relationships. His death speaks of the crucifixion of beauty in the world. His resurrection expresses the hope that what has become ugly in us will be transformed again.

Beauty emanates from the very heart of life. This is not to say that beauty is as an end in itself. It is one of the emanations of the mystery of God and needs to be experienced in relation to the others. A beauty that is isolated from wisdom or love is not a true expression of beauty. Only in the most superficial of senses can we refer to people as beautiful if at the same time they are unjust. It is like the incongruity of the Nazi love for beautiful music in the death camps of Europe in the Second World War, and the use of their Jewish victims as the principal musicians. True beauty and love serve one another, as do love and mystery, and strength and wisdom, for all of the emanations are one.

In the Old Testament King David is associated with the beautiful music and poetry of the Psalms, but beauty is not allowed to stand on its own. This is not a spirituality of aesthetics. Rather, the Psalter's beauty is given to serve wisdom and love. Likewise they are given to serve beauty.

Anything else leads to a type of heart disease at the centre of the human mystery. If our true passion for beauty fails, so does our energy for wisdom, so does our desire for justice.

The prophet Isaiah promises a restoration of Jerusalem's beauty. Her wilderness will be 'like Eden' and 'her desert like the garden of the Lord'.[56] But this can only be, he says, 'if you offer your food to the hungry and satisfy the needs of the afflicted'.[57] It is a fallacy to think that we can have true beauty and at the same time ignore justice. It would be like calling Christ the perfect Art of God while disregarding what he has to say about the purpose of his ministry, 'to bring good news to the poor . . . to let the oppressed go free'.[58] The Psalmist says, 'steadfast love and faithfulness will meet; righteousness and peace will kiss each other'.[59] So it is with beauty and justice, and with wisdom and love. They are inseparably interwoven. If justice is torn from beauty, we are left not with beauty but with a hollow mask of beauty.

Within every human being are doors that lead into the inner sanctuary of God's beauty. These are 'ancient doors' like the doors of the temple, and what we are encouraged to do by the Psalms is to be 'doorkeepers'.[60] We open the ancient doors not just for ourselves but for one another and for the world. When I enter the inner sanctuary of beauty within my own being, I bring not only myself but the whole world of which I am a part. As the Jewish mystics say, from within us we can release sparks of beauty into the world, there to kindle other sparks of beauty.

Jesus' words, 'the kingdom of God is within you', equally can be translated 'the kingdom of God is among you'.[61] That which is deep within us waiting to be recovered is also deep between us and among us in the whole of life. Our own healing is part of the world's healing. And our own recovery of beauty can be happening even in the midst of what may appear not very beautiful. The story is told of a rabbi who entered paradise. As he approached the temple all he saw were some of the great sages of Judaism sitting around very ordinary tables studying the Torah. The rabbi, disappointed with what he saw, thought, 'Is this all there is to paradise?', at which point he heard a voice saying, 'You are mistaken. The wise men are not in paradise. Paradise is in the wise men.'

The beauty of the kingdom of God is within us and among us. We are invited to release this hidden treasure.

Words for Meditation

'Strength and beauty are in your sanctuary' *(Psalm 96:6)*.

5

The Creativity of the Self

The genitals are associated with creativity and pro-creativity.[1] They represent the origins, genesis or source of new life. They are related to conception and birth. In Ezekiel's vision of the cloud of unknowing, in which he glimpses the mystery of God in human form, he sees what is like a fire coming from the loins of God.[2] It has the appearance of a great brightness. It is like 'gleaming amber', says Ezekiel.[3] God is the source of life. All life comes forth, as it were, from the fire of God's loins. The Genesis picture is of the world coming into being from the light of God. It is the life-force of the whole of creation. It is, as St John says, the light that 'enlightens every person coming into the world'.[4] Life has been expressed into being from the mystery of God. All things have issued forth from God's life.

Ezekiel's imagery is masculine, but in the Book of Job we find a feminine parallel. Job envisages creation coming forth from the womb of God.[5] God like a mother gives birth to life. But whether the imagery used is masculine or feminine, the Scriptures are pointing to a vital connection between the mystery of God and the mystery of creation. God's being is not infinitely separated from creation's being. Rather, creation in all its physicalness is viewed as issuing forth from God. The words used in Genesis to describe the birth of Adam's son are that he was born in Adam's 'likeness, according to his image'.[6] These are exactly the words used to describe the birth of humanity. 'Let us make humankind in our image,' says God, 'according to our likeness.'[7] The implication is not that humanity is made out of nothing but that humanity is born from the essence of God.

John Scotus Eriugena describes creation as coming into being from 'the secret recesses of the Father's substance', and says that it is 'always being born'.[8] As Ecclesiasticus says, 'God is the all'.[9] God's life is the essence of all life. Without God's life there would be no life. St Paul says that 'from God and through God and to God are all things'.[10] Similarly, the Wisdom of Solomon says, 'God's immortal spirit is in all things'.[11] God's 'spirit' is the very spark of life.

Ezekiel's vision of the fire of God's loins influenced later Jewish mysticism, which came to speak of the holy sparks of God that are in all things. In the thirteenth-century kabbalistic text, the *Zohar*, the light that is in all things is described as sparkling forth from the eternal and invisible light of God:

> I have seen that all those sparks flash from the High
> Spark,
> hidden of all hidden . . .
> All those lights are connected:
> this light to that light, that light to this light,
> one shining into the other,
> inseparable, one from the other. . . .
> All those sparks and all those lights sparkle from the
> Holy Ancient One,
> concealed of all concealed, the High Spark.[12]

The more alive something is the more full it is of the holy sparks. And the more full it is of life the more sacred it is. Creation is not simply set in motion from afar to self-perpetuate itself. Rather, as the *Zohar* teaches, it is constantly streaming forth from the light of God:

> Every single day, a ray of that light shines into the world,
>   keeping everything alive;
> with that ray God feeds the world.[13]

John the Baptist says of Jesus that he will baptise 'with the Holy Spirit and fire'.[14] Jesus comes to make us more alive, not with a light that is somehow foreign to creation but with a fire that is the very life of creation. It is the light of life from which we have cut ourselves off or become distant.

This perception of light is developed over the centuries in the Christian mystical tradition. The twelfth-century German mystic Hildegaard of Bingen records in one of her revelations:

> I, the highest and fiery power, have kindled every living spark. . . . I flame above the beauty of the fields; I shine in the waters; in the sun, the moon and the stars, I burn. And by means of the airy wind, I stir everything into quickness with a certain invisible life which sustains all. . . . I, the fiery power, lie hidden in these things and they blaze from me.[15]

William Blake, in his Felpham vision on the south coast of England, saw what he called 'particles bright' forming the shape of a human being.[16] The life of humanity and of the whole of creation is on fire from God. Without this fire nothing would be.

The secular perspective of the Western world has wanted to say that we simply come forth from the earth, or from the cosmos, and that we are sustained by the earth's waters and vegetation and various life forms. To say that we are born of the earth does not exclude also saying that we are born of God. We have come through our mothers and fathers and from the earth, and we are dependent upon the vegetable and animal world for survival, but in all of these are the holy sparks of God. The food and drink that we receive from the earth are life-giving precisely because they contain the vital fire of God's life. In fact the more strengthening and the more satisfying they are the fuller they are of the Holy Spirit.

The belief that all life comes forth from the mystery of God, combined with the belief that our bodies are made in the image of God, led the Jewish tradition to affirm the sacredness of the human body, including the holiness of the genitals. The genitals are associated with the origins of life, and ultimately with the genesis of all life in God. The Jewish practice of circumcision relates to this belief. In the circumcision of a male child the foreskin is cut away from the phallus. 'You shall circumcise the flesh of your fore-skins,' says God, 'and it shall be a sign of the covenant between you and me.'[17] The understanding that developed in Jewish mystical practice was that the foreskin represented a covering over of the phallus. It symbolised for them humanity's tendency to cover over or to forget that our origins are in the phallus or the loins of God. Jewish covenantal practice was designed to remember and to disclose that the seminal force of life is God. The Book of Deuteronomy makes the same point by using feminine imagery, when it says, 'You have forgotten the One who gave you birth.'[18] It is a call to remember that, although we come through the loins of our ancestors, ultimately our life is of God.

Edwin Muir, in his poem 'The Journey Back', speaks of the need to 'seek the beginnings, learn from whence you came'.[19] In his imagination he travels 'from place to place' in the past and from one generation to the next in his family line, trying to find what he calls 'the secret place where is my home'. But the linear search takes him only so far. What we require, he says, is a 'blessing' in order to discover the hidden road, the one we do not know. It is on that road, he says, that we will hear 'a music underground'. It is like a subterranean river running through all things. In his autobiography he calls it 'a universal unchanging underground' from which all life comes forth.[20]

The question of our deepest place of origin occupies Muir throughout his autobiography, which he concludes by saying:

> As I look back on the part of the mystery which is my own life, my own fable, what I am most aware of is that we receive more than we can ever give; we receive it from the past, on which we draw with every breath, but also – and this is a point of faith – from the Source of the mystery itself, by means which religious people call Grace.[21]

This is Muir's way of pointing to the same mystery that the Jewish covenantal practice of circumcision is pointing to. Our deepest life source in every moment is God.

At different points in Christian history, if there had been a religious ritual in relation to the male genitals, it might well have taken the form not of circumcision but of emasculation. Again and again the Christian tradition has failed to make a profound connection between our spirituality and our humanity, or between the mystery of God, on the one hand, and the mystery of the human body, on the other.

Little attention is given to the fact that Jesus' full humanity would have included the experience of genital erection and sexual attraction. The male experience of an erect phallus in the night or in the early hours of the morning is a universal experience from boyhood to manhood. At the simplest level it represents a renewing of deep physical energy in us. Phallic erection is also the response to sexual attraction. It signifies vitality and a capacity to express the seed of new life. Genital activity is fundamental to the mystery of creation's existence and of humanity's continuity. If we say that Jesus, who reveals true humanity to us, knew nothing of sexual energy in himself, what are we saying about our sexuality? Are we saying that it is somehow not truly human or that it is opposed to the nature of God, our maker and the maker of all creation? Are we wanting to suggest that the sexual principle, deep in the matter and lifeblood of creation, has an origin other than God?

James Nelson, the distinguished American theologian who has given attention to the relationship between spirituality and sexuality, makes the point that the Church has not always been in a state of denial about the sexuality of Jesus.[22] In *Sexuality and the Sacred* he describes the ways in which Renaissance art, for instance, consciously incorporates genital imagery into its depictions of Christ. In scenes of the incarnation and epiphany, for example, Mary can be found spreading the infant's thighs so that the magi can see the true humanity of the Christ-child. In certain depictions of the passion Jesus cups his hands over his genitals at the point of death, the artist thereby signifying that Christ's source of life is now hidden. In other crucifixion scenes there are unabashed signs of phallic erection in Jesus, symbolising the divine strength for new life that will not be overcome by death's threatening powers.

Such art reflects an integration that has been lacking in much of our Christian history. The cost of not integrating our sexual energies with our spiritual yearnings has been enormous. It has led either to a suppressing of our God-given sexual desires, with the result that these become confused and guilt-ridden, or to a type of schizophrenic division of our lives between the spiritual realm and the realm of sexual relationship and passion.

William Blake, who believed that our sexuality is a form of divine energy, complained that religion, with its 'Abhorrence' of the sexual, resulted in a 'withered up' form of humanity.[23] Instead of making us more truly human, religion was sapping our humanity. 'Go to these Fiends of Righteousness,' he writes. 'Tell them to obey their Humanities, and not to pretend to Holiness.'[24] It is a false holiness that denies the sexual energies that God has woven into the depths of our beings. Echoing the Jewish mystical tradition's affirmation of the whole of the human body, Blake contends that the 'Establishment of Truth' in the realm of human sexuality depends not 'on Virginity' but 'on Circumcision'.[25] A fullness of humanity is found not through a refusing or suppressing of our sexual energies, namely 'Virginity', but through a cutting away of what covers over the true origins of life and revealing the sacredness of the sexual, namely 'Circumcision'.

Mircea Eliade, the historian of religion, claims that, with the exception of the modern world, 'sexuality has everywhere and always been a hierophany', that is a revealing of the sacred.[26] In other words, the sexual dimension of our beings and relationships can lead us into a sense of the sacred at levels deeper than conscious understanding. The functions and feelings of the genitals can be a mode of revelation. They can reveal to us something of the ineffable mystery that is at the heart of our lives and of all life.

To believe that we are made in the image of God is to affirm the essential goodness of the fire that is in our own loins. Blake, for instance, speaks about *our* 'bright loins'.[27] From the passion of our loins our children are born. From the passion of our creative depths comes forth what has never been before. In our relationships, in our art forms, in the building of a just society together or in the creation of peace between nations, we have the capacity to conceive of new beginnings and to give birth to what is utterly original.

Creativity, as represented by the genitals, has its rhythms of activity and restfulness. In relation to men we tend to associate the phallus in its erect state with creative potential. The reality, however, is that for most of the time the penis is not erect with a readiness for hard and explosive phallic achievement. Rather, it is soft and limp. In fact it looks rather feeble, nothing like a source of strength for new life. But unless the phallus is inactive most of the time it will not rise to the creative occasion. Similarly, of course, with the regeneration of seed in a man or in the development of the ovum in a woman, long periods of apparent inactivity prepare for the relatively brief moments of fertility and conception. There is a rhythm to creativity deep in the mystery of the human body that we need to learn from in all of the creativities of our lives. The times of stillness and reflection are as essential to the birth of new ideas and beginnings as the moments of intense engagement and action.

The Creativity of the Self

True creativity is also something that calls for a com-
mingling of strengths between people, rather than the exercising of a one-sided power over another. In the case of a
man and woman coming together genitally, the strength of
the erect phallus is vital but so is the strength of moisture in
the vagina and the open moving forward to engage and
draw the phallus further in. Unless there is a merging of
genital strengths the relationship becomes non-mutual and
potentially abusive. The sacred text of the human body tells
us that it is vital that the energies we bring to creativity
awaken and invite the creative energies of the other.
Creativity is not a unilateral energy but a relational energy.

The Scriptures say, 'be fruitful and multiply'.[28] The
Jewish mystics sometimes poke fun at religion's tendency
to teach obedience to God's commands, while at the same
time giving the impression that we are not to have pleasure
in doing so. The religious message becomes 'be fruitful and
multiply', but don't enjoy it.

I was once told by a Baptist minister with a twinkle in his
eye why it is that members of his own denomination do not
believe in making love standing up. 'The reason', he said,
'is because it might lead to dancing.' There has been a
terrible fear across all of the Christian denominations
about abandoning ourselves to pleasure. Where does this
fear come from?

An eighteenth-century rabbi in the kabbalistic tradition
recounted how he came to see pleasure and holiness not as
opposed to each other but as one:

I once heard a chaste man bemoaning the fact that sexual
union is inherently pleasurable. He preferred that there
be no physical pleasure at all, so that he could unite with
his wife solely to fulfil the command of his Creator:

'Be fruitful and multiply.' . . . I took this to mean that one should sanctify one's thought by eliminating any intention of feeling physical pleasure. One should bemoan the fact that pleasurable sensation is inherent to this act. If only it were not so! Sometime later, God favoured me with a gift of grace, granting me under-standing of the essence of sexual holiness. The holiness derives precisely from feeling the pleasure. This secret is wondrous, deep, and awesome.[29]

'The holiness derives precisely from feeling the pleasure.' The rabbi had come to see that the depth of pleasure in any action is in direct proportion to the holiness of the action. The pleasure of sexual union is an unparalleled pleasure. In the kabbalistic tradition it is therefore a most holy action. As a thirteenth-century kabbalist said, 'The union of man and woman, when it is right, is the secret of civilisation. Thereby, one becomes a partner with God in the act of Creation. This is the secret meaning of the saying of the sages: "When a man unites with his wife in holiness, the divine presence is between them."'[30]

This did not give way to a lawless self-indulgence or licentiousness in the kabbalistic tradition. There were strict boundaries to marital relationship, precisely because sexual union was sacred. Sexual union, however, needs to be named as a sacred pleasure rather than shamefully unmen-tioned in our family lives and religious communities. The Prophecy of Isaiah says of God's anointed one that 'faith-fulness is the belt around his loins'.[31] Faithfulness is not a chastity belt that cuts off our sexual energies. Rather, it channels them. Our sexuality is like a rich stream that flows deep within us and between us. It will remain deep and rich, however, only when it is bounded by the steep

88

banks of commitment and faithfulness. A fallacy of our modern age is the belief that the river of our sexuality can be both deep and unbounded.

Always in the Jewish tradition there is an emphasis on the essential unity of the emanations. The pleasure of sexual union is not merely a genital pleasure, but a pleasure in harmony with the other emanations, with love and beauty, for instance, or with wisdom and mystery. The fire of our loins is given to serve the love that we have for another. It is offered in reverence for the mystery and the beauty that are in the other. Similarly, the other emanations are given to serve the fire of creativity in us. The beauty and love of our partner kindles the flame of our sexuality, just as wisdom and its limitless imagination can guide us and free us in our lovemaking. The picture from Proverbs of the conception of the universe is of wisdom playfully releasing the creative energies of God into an infinity of expression and embodiment.[32]

A delight in the passion of lovemaking is clearly expressed in the biblical tradition. In the Song of Songs the bridegroom speaks of being 'drunk with love'.[33] And the bride says, 'Let my beloved come to his garden, and eat its choicest fruits.'[34] The feast of tasting love in one another is a shared passion. 'With great delight', she says, 'I sat in his shadow, and his fruit was sweet to my taste.'[35] The religious inhibitions around naming genital pleasure as good and of God have led to a tendency to spiritualise this greatest of love poems. Implied in this is a denial that our bodies, in all their parts, are an expression of the mystery of God.

The bride describes the beloved knocking at her door, desiring to enter. He 'thrust his hand into the opening,' she says, 'and my inmost being yearned for him. I arose to open to my beloved, and my hands dripped with myrrh, my fingers with liquid myrrh, upon the handles of the bolt. I opened to my beloved.'[36] Such a passage speaks of the pleasure of the passion of our loins in sensuous and full-blooded ways. The sap of life and the moisture of sexual energy are celebrated in the poem. Its depths are achieved precisely because the spiritual and the physical are not torn apart but inseparably interwoven. When we regard our body or the body of another simply as flesh we cheapen the sexuality of our beings and lose sight of the spiritual depths that are within us. Pleasure is greatest precisely when we touch the spiritual dimension that is within the physical-ness of our bodies.

Why is it that we have tended to dismiss words like 'pleasure' and 'delight' from our religious vocabulary? Eriugena, in the Celtic tradition, speaks in exactly the opposite terms. Heaven, he says, is where there is delight and pleasure. Hell, on the other hand, is where there is no delighting and no pleasure.[37] The experience of true pleasure is about being reconnected to the delights of Eden at the beginning and heart of life. As the nineteenth-century poet Gerard Manley Hopkins says, 'What is all this juice and all this joy? A strain of the earth's sweet being in the beginning in Eden garden.'[38]

The Scriptures state clearly that we are made from 'the seed of man and the pleasure of marriage'.[39] Just as clearly they call us to be aware of the pain of creativity. 'Do not forget the birth pangs of your mother', says Ecclesiasticus.[40] The most precious relationships and creativities of our lives invite us not simply into pleasure but into the cost of struggle and growing together. There is a delight in conception, whether that be the conception of children or of creative work and expression, but there is also the sweat and labour and tears of bringing creativity to birth. Holy pleasure is not without holy pain. To open ourselves to a depth of creativity in relationship, to give ourselves for example to a true intimacy of sexual union, is to enter a realm of vulnerability that exposes the core of our being to another. It is for this reason that in the great love poem we find the refrain, 'do not stir up or awaken love until it is ready'.[41] The holy pleasure of intimacy is not a cheap pleasure and cannot be hurried. Its full richness is forged only with time and with trust.

To say that all things come forth from the loins of God is also to say that all things share in the essence of God's goodness. 'And God saw everything that he had made, and indeed, it was very good,' says Genesis.[42] This is a foundational truth in our biblical tradition and it speaks of an eternal reality. Creation is forever being born and its essence is forever seen by God as good.

To see creation as constantly becoming is to be transported 'from a place where there is nothing new to a place where there is nothing old,' says the Kabbalah, 'where heaven and earth rejoice as at the moment of creation'.[43] To see things with the perspective of creation's first moment is to see the goodness that is deep within everything that is being born. The Genesis account says that the man and the woman 'were both naked and were not ashamed'.[44] It is only after their failure that they make 'loincloths for themselves'.[45] They cover their loins and the goodness of the source of their life and of all life.

There is no doubt in any of us that we have failed. There is much doubt, however, about the goodness of our human bodies and our sexuality. Do we choose to live out of the shame of our failures and the fear of failing again, or do we choose to live in the grace of the forgiveness that invites us to look deeper than our sin to the goodness of what has been planted by God at the core of our beings? The goodness that God forever sees being born in creation is not simply out there in the external realm of nature but deep in the inner nature of our beings and deep in our capacity to give birth to what has never been before.

To say that we are made in the image of the goodness of God is not to be naive about what has gone wrong. Similarly, to say that the human body, including the genitals, is essentially good is not to be blind to the ways in which the body's goodness has been distorted in us. In an age obsessed with genital sex we do not have to look far, either outside of ourselves or within ourselves, to be aware of twisted sexual desires. As one Hasidic rabbi taught, although the genitals are a small part of the human body they can mislead the entire body. A distortion of our sexual passions can throw into imbalance the whole of our life.

Especially in relation to the phallus we know how what is created good can be perverted into what is wrong. Many slang terms for the penis have clear associations with domination and force. The male organ is referred to as a prick or a rod, and as a gun firing bullets. Genesis speaks of the goodness of all that has been created. It also provides us, however, with the first account of genital abuse. The men of Sodom, instead of welcoming strangers into their city, attempt to exert power over them by trying to sexually abuse them.[46] We have witnessed in places of collective violence and ethnic cleansing in our world how the sacred strength of the phallus becomes instead an unholy power for domination and terror.

Such abuses of human sexuality can seem irredeemable. The evil that sin gives rise to often appears to have a type of omnipotence about it. As we have noted, the Revelation of St John the Divine describes evil's resources as emerging from what seems to be a bottomless pit. The biblical perspective, however, is that evil has no ultimate power. The Wisdom of Solomon speaks of Hades as 'powerless'[47] and St John the Divine's vision is of evil eventually burning itself out. Whereas goodness comes forth from the loins of the One who is eternal, evil and the abuse of creative energies have no foundation in eternity. They have no eternal source.

This is not to suggest that the Bible downplays the threatening power of evil and the forces that are opposed to life and creativity. Ezekiel's prophecy includes a vision of death's destructiveness on a massive scale. It is the valley of dry bones. 'It was full of bones', he says, 'and they were very dry.'[48] The picture is of the human capacity for self-destruction. It is a picture of desolation and hopelessness on an enormous scale. The valley is entirely dry. There is not a sign of life's moisture and fertility. The Spirit of the Lord asks Ezekiel, 'Can these bones live?' Is this not the question that is forever being asked in situations of horrendous devastation and abuse in our world where nations are torn apart and communities are annihilated by hatred? Is this not the question we ask in our own lives when our energies to create and to conceive of new beginnings are used instead to destroy or to waste the gifts of life and love that we have been given? And yet the Spirit says to Ezekiel, 'Prophesy to these bones, and say to them: . . . I will cause spirit to enter you, and you shall live.' God's sparks of life are both creating and redeeming.

Later in the Prophecy of Ezekiel there is another vision. Ezekiel sees a fountain surging up from the heart of the temple. Life-giving waters issue forth from the fountain, and the river gushes out of the gateways of the temple. Wherever it flows there is life. Stagnant waters become fresh and the river becomes so deep and fast-flowing that Ezekiel is unable to stand in it. On the riverbank fruit trees grow up and the Spirit says to Ezekiel, 'they will bear fresh fruit every month, because the water for them flows from the sanctuary. Their fruit will be for food, and their leaves for healing.'[49]

Ezekiel's vision is of the flow of God's life being both creative and redemptive. The fruit is for food, he says, and the leaves are for healing. The fountain of God is for the making of life as well as for the remaking of life. The biblical tradition begins with a description of God's Spirit brooding 'over the face of the waters' to bring forth life.[50] At the end of the Scriptures, the created world now broken with suffering and death is being re-created by God. 'See', says the Spirit, 'I am making all things new.'[51] Throughout the whole of the Scriptures the creative and the re-creative presence of God again and again are pointed to. 'I have made', as the Prophecy of Isaiah says, 'and I will save'.[52] If the fountain of God's life were to be blocked up, not only would the flow of God's healing graces be stopped but the gift of life itself would cease.

In meditating on the theme of God as the fountain of life, four women reflected on different aspects of the mystery. The first woman saw in her meditation a fountain gushing forth from a fathomless well. Its spray consisted of a myriad of droplets shooting in all directions. The droplets brought forth life wherever they fell. The second woman saw in the bursting streams of the fountain the birds of the air, the fish of the sea and all of earth's creatures issuing forth from the waters of God. The third woman saw herself in one of the streams. The fountain's waters were gushing into her and soaking her with vitality. The fourth woman danced with abandonment in the very source of the fountain, but then found herself sitting out on the edge of a wall frightened by its force and fearful of re-entering the water. These four meditations speak in different ways of the flow of God's life surging up, not only from the heart of creation but from the depths of each one of us. The fourth meditation speaks also of the fear that is in us at the power and the energy of this flow.

To be made in the image of God is to be made in the image of the One who is both creating and redeeming. Within us is a mighty fountain gushing with power. It can create and heal life, but equally it can destroy and tear life apart. The genitals represent that dimension of who we are. The surging fountain within us can give birth to new life for the world and can passionately heal what has been wounded by failures and faithlessness. Jesus says, 'from your inner being will flow rivers of living water'.[53] But the inner fountain also has the capacity of a destructive flood that can spoil creative vitalities and channel our energies into bitterness or wrong instead of healing.

What is our desire? The Scriptures say, 'Let anyone who wishes take the water of life as a gift.'[54] The fountain at the heart of our being is a gift, offered not once but in every moment of life. As the Prophecy of Isaiah says, 'I am about to do a new thing; now it springs forth, do you not perceive it?'[55] God is forever the fountain of life. Now it springs forth within us. Do we not perceive it?

Words for Meditation

'With you is the fountain of life' *(Psalm 36:9)*.

6

THE ETERNITY OF THE SELF

The legs of the human body are associated with eternity and glory. They are like the pillars of the human form. St Paul says, 'Do you not know that you are the temple of God?'[1] The glory and the eternity of God are the pillars of the temple of our being.

The Second Book of Chronicles, in describing the Jerusalem Temple, says that there were two main pillars.[2] The one on the right was called 'Jachin', which means solid foundation. The one on the left was called 'Boaz', which means glorious strength. In time the Jewish mystics referred to these as the pillars undergirding the mystery of our being.

The Temple was a sacred site associated with the mystery of God's presence. It was identified with wisdom and divine strength. It was an embodiment of beauty and, as we have seen, a symbol of the source or fountain of life. Undergirding these were the twin pillars. They represented the eternity and the glory that uphold the temple of the universe itself. If somehow these were taken away, the temple of reality would collapse.

The universe 'stands firm in God's glory', says Ecclesiasticus.[3] And as the Psalmist says, 'Before the mountains were brought forth, or ever you had formed the earth, from everlasting to everlasting you are God.'[4] The mystery of our being and of all being is rooted in the eternal glory that precedes the formation of the earth's mountains and all creation. We are of the 'King of glory',[5] and therefore, as the Celtic tradition likes to say, we are princes and princesses of glory. That is our hidden and truest identity. The reality, of course, is that we live at a distance from the foundations of our being. Like Jacob, who walked with a limp after wrestling with God's angel in the night, we walk with an unsteadiness of spirit.[6]

The outer temple of life is passing. Solomon's Temple was destroyed in the sixth century BC. Similarly, the outward temples of our bodies are fading, as is the temple of creation itself. One day it will be no more. But the inner temple, the temple 'not made with hands', as the Scriptures say, is forever held in place by the eternal glory of God.[7]

The pillars of that inner temple are our true stability. They are at the very core of our beings. The One who is above us and greater than all things is the One who is within us and the foundation of all life. As an eleventh-century French mystic says, 'Gazing into the Throne of Glory means descending into oneself in order to ascend to the Infinite.'[8] The 'withinness' and the 'aboveness' of God, traditionally referred to as the divine immanence and transcendence, are pointing to identical experiences of God. We place the mystery of God 'furthest outward', says Martin Buber, precisely because our experience of the mystery is the 'most inward'.[9] William Blake speaks of a universe within us. 'In every bosom a Universe expands,' he says.[10] It is the universe of God's presence. It is without beginning and without end.

We know what it is like to lie on the ground gazing upwards into the glory and infinity of the sky. We are overwhelmed by its endlessness and its infinity of lights. Are we also aware of the inner universe and its infinity? The outer universe is a sign of the everlasting world of glory within us. The boundless depths of our inner world, says Blake, are 'starry and glorious'.[11] He calls these 'the depths of wondrous worlds'.[12] 'What is Above is Within', he says. There are 'Heavens and Earths' within us.[13]

To point to the eternity of the unseen universe within us is not to belittle the physical universe or the outward particulars of day-to-day life. As Blake writes elsewhere, 'Eternity is in love with the productions of time.'[14] The outward details of our lives and relationships, like the physical glory of creation, are sacred because they are expressions of the eternal reality of God. The challenge is to see the union of the spiritual and the physical, to discern the everlasting in the passing forms of outward life. It is, as Blake says:

> To see a World in a Grain of Sand
> And a Heaven in a Wild Flower
> Hold Infinity in the palm of your hand
> And Eternity in an hour.[15]

It is not just in our own inner temple then that we are to be alert to the glory and eternity of God. It is in one another and in the vast temple of creation. 'The whole earth is full of God's glory,' says Isaiah.[16]

The Prophecy of Ezekiel sees the Jerusalem Temple filled with a cloud of glory. It is the bright cloud of the mystery of God's presence. 'The court', says Ezekiel, 'was full of the brightness of the glory of the Lord.'[17] This is not a vision simply of one particular place, but of a glory that is every-where present. Holy places and holy times are like sacraments that lead us into seeing the holiness of every place and every time. As Ezekiel sees in another vision, the glory of God fills all things like the sun's light rising from the east. 'The earth shone with his glory,' says Ezekiel.[18] Ecclesiasticus speaks of the whole of creation 'sparkling' with God's light,[19] while St Paul says, 'there is a glory of the sun, and a glory of the moon, and a glory of the stars'.[20] Each created thing is an expression of the eternal light. It is a manifestation of what the Scottish poet Kenneth White calls the 'glow-flow' that courses through the veins of creation.[21] As the Jewish mystics say, it 'drenches' the trees of the earth with glory.[22] It saturates life with sacredness.

The Celtic stream of spirituality has been characterised by this type of alertness to glory. As George MacLeod, the founder of the modern-day Iona Community, used to say, all things are 'shot through with spirit'. Creation is 'vibrant with the everlasting'.[23] Similarly, the ancient prayers of the Hebrides, known as the *Carmina Gadelica*, celebrate the interwovenness of the spiritual and the material. The glory of God is glimpsed in all the things of earth and heaven:

> Thou King of the moon,
> Thou King of the sun,
> Thou King of the planets,
> Thou King of the stars,
> Thou King of the globe,
> Thou King of the sky,
> Oh! lovely Thy countenance
> Thou beauteous Beam.[24]

To see something of the hidden glory of God in the lights of creation led the Celtic tradition towards a form of sun and moon reverencing. As one of the *Carmina Gadelica* prayers put it:

Echo of the Soul

When I see the new moon,
It becomes me to lift mine eye,
It becomes me to bend my knee,
It becomes me to bow my head.[25]

To bend one's knee or to bow one's head to the moon, a practice that was widespread in the Hebrides of Scotland until early in the nineteenth century, was of course regarded by many outside the Celtic tradition as pagan or pantheistic. Within the Celtic tradition, however, it was viewed as a form of Christ-mysticism. It was not the light of the moon that was being worshipped but the Light within the light. The glory of God was seen as piercing the thin veil that divides heaven and earth. To reverence the light of creation was, at the same time, to be looking deeper than creation to the eternal glory that is forever breaking through.

A similar distinction can be found among the Jewish mystics. The lights of creation were seen as the clothing or the adornments of God. The Hasidim used the analogy of a man desiring a woman who is beautifully clothed. Although he will be aware of her splendid garments, for they carry her scent and express her vivacity, the focus of his desire is the woman, not her clothing. A man who does not desire the woman, on the other hand, will notice only the beauty of her clothing. So it is with the person who desires God. The focus of the desire is not creation but the divine presence that creation expresses. The Jewish mystics refer to this as a yearning to see 'the great shining of the world's inwardness'.[26]

Early in the Jewish tradition, Jacob dreams of angels of light ascending and descending a ladder that connects heaven and earth. When he awakes Jacob says, 'Surely God is in this place and I did not know it! . . . This is none other than the house of God, and this is the gate of heaven.'[27] Jacob names the place 'Bethel', which means 'House of God'.

In nearly every religious tradition the problem with naming particular places as sacred or holy is that we have given the impression, and sometimes even have come to believe, that the glory of God's presence is somehow contained by these places and times. We find this tendency being addressed in the Christian tradition as early as the writing of the Gospels. In the story of the transfiguration, when Peter, James and John on a mountain top see the light of Christ's glory, and the glory of Moses and Elijah, Peter says to Jesus, 'let us make three dwellings, one for you, one for Moses, and one for Elijah'.[28] Peter's words represent the religious tendency to try to locate in place what is always beyond containment and beyond expression. As Solomon prays at the completion of the first temple in Jerusalem, 'Even heaven and the highest heaven cannot contain you, much less this house that I have built.'[29]

God's glory knows no boundaries. It is deep in the foundations of creation and at the heart of every human being. Certainly we have been more aware of glory at particular moments in our lives. In certain places the doors of our inner senses open more readily, but the gate that leads into the place of God's glory is everywhere present. Our 'holy' sites are signs of the hidden glory that is in all things. The gift of grace is given to open our eyes to this glory. As the Jewish mystics say, 'Happy is the one whose eyes shine from this secret, in this world and the world that is coming.'[30]

The nineteenth-century poet Gerard Manley Hopkins writes, 'The world is charged with the grandeur of God'.[31] Sometimes, he says, 'It will flame out, like shining from shook foil'. At other times its self-disclosure is subtle, 'It gathers to a greatness, like the ooze of oil crushed.' These showings of 'the grandeur of God' issue up from deep within, from what Hopkins refers to as the 'instress' of the divine glory in creation. 'There lives the dearest freshness deep down things,' he says. The poet Kenneth White speaks of 'fields of in-being' and of a type of 'ingoing knowing'. 'The deepest is the most alive,' he says.[32] The deeper we move in relation to any created thing the closer we come to the eternal vitality of God.

Blake's way of putting it is to say that the universe 'opens like a flower from the Earth's centre: In which is Eternity'.[33] He imagines that just as the physical universe is still expanding 'going forward to Eternity', so the 'Circumference' of the inner universe is forever opening further into the infinity of God. The centre of our being 'has Eternal States', and, as he says in his poem 'Jerusalem', 'these States we now explore'.[34] The purpose of the poem, like much of his poetry, is to discover further the universe of the soul and to know it as the place of our deepest vitality. As the Prophecy of Isaiah says, we are to take 'root downward' if we are to bear 'fruit upward'.[35] Within us are stems reaching into the life-giving glory of God. These eternal roots have not been severed in us, but they are forever needing to be rediscovered.

Teilhard de Chardin, a great Christian mystic and scientist of the twentieth century, said that each expression of life is like a cone with its point established beneath in the invisible realm of God's eternity. At its surface it opens to reveal the depth of life's glory. A man meditating on this theme of glory at the heart of life also saw a conical shape. Its tip was the beginning of time, the first moment. He saw it, like a funnel, filling up. Everything in the cone of life was related, the light of the solar system and the light of human life all interconnected. The tip of the cone and the beginning of all things is in the eternal glory of God. The Jewish mystics refer to this as 'the secret concealed point' from which all life emanates.[36]

Although 'the world is charged with the grandeur of God', as Hopkins says, our vision of the glory is impaired. In part this is because our inner faculties of perception have become dulled and distorted. When we are not alert within ourselves we will not be aware of the glory, even when it is glaring at us in the face like the brilliance of the rising sun breaking through the darkness of the early morning. But our vision is dimmed also because the glory is polluted or driven down. 'Generations have trod, have trod, have trod,' writes Hopkins, 'and all is seared with trade; bleared, smeared with toil.' Our abuse of the environment, and the way we have built our cities and developed our lifestyles, has trampled earth's glory. 'The soil is bare now,' writes Hopkins, 'nor can foot feel, being shod.'[37] We have walked over earth's glory with boots of insensitivity.

The parallels between trampling creation's splendour and effacing the glory that is in humanity are widespread. In practice they are inseparably linked. What we do to the earth is what we do to ourselves. The way we treat the body of creation is, in the end, the way we treat the body of humanity. If we increasingly cut ourselves off from the glory that is in the earth and in one another, we will come to live as if the glory is not there. The less we allow ourselves to be touched by that glory the less we will believe that glory is the foundation of life.

We have all witnessed, even if it is only from afar, terrible abuses of life's glory. A haunting image came for me in documentary footage of a home for mentally ill children in Moldavia. A twelve-year-old girl, physically stunted through lack of nutrition and proper care, had spent ten years in a cage no larger than six feet square. The untrained and under-resourced staff said that she was happier in the cage. 'Outside of it', they said, 'she would run wild.' Instances of such imprisonment of glory and blindness of perception are countless, and in many cases far worse even than this. We do not have to look outside our own countries or beyond our own families and lives to know that glory has been imprisoned and held down in all sorts of ways. How is it to be liberated again?

'If the doors of our perceptions were cleansed,' says Blake, 'then everything would appear to us as it is: infinite.'[38] Edwin Muir, in his poem 'The Transfiguration', envisions a grace of healing that issues up from the ground of being to transfigure humanity and its inner sight, 'the source of all our seeing rinsed and cleansed', he says.[39] If our inner vision were restored, we would glimpse again what he calls 'the unseeable One glory of the everlasting world perpetually at work'. We would know that our own physicalness, like the matter of all creation, is 'made of immortal substance'. Instead of the dirt or 'soot' beneath our feet, which we fear to be the deepest reality, we would see that deeper still is 'the stone clean at the heart as on the starting-day'. Muir is pointing to a grace that reconnects us to the true ground of our being.

In his autobiography, Muir describes a birth within himself at the age of thirty-five of a new way of seeing. Not only does it open his eyes to the glory that is around him and ahead of him in his life, but to the glory that he had only half noticed in the past without actually seeing it:

> I realized that I must live over again the years which I had lived wrongly . . . I went over my life . . . like a man

who after travelling a long, featureless road suddenly realizes that, at this point or that, he had noticed almost without knowing it, with the corner of his eye, some extraordinary object, some rare treasure, yet in his sleep-walking had gone on, consciously aware only of the blank road flowing back beneath his feet. These objects . . . were still patiently waiting at the point where I had first ignored them, and my full gaze could take in things which an absent glance had once passed over unseeingly, so that life I had wasted was returned to me . . . I did not feel so much that I was rediscovering the world of life as that I was discovering it for the first time.[40]

The grace of new sight not only liberates us for the present and the future, but can be part of redeeming our past.

The Jewish mystics believed that the light of the Messiah would reveal the hidden light of the universe. He would disclose the glory that is the foundation of life. The Christian tradition similarly believes that in the light of Christ, the Messiah, we see the light of life, the glory that undergirds our being and all being. Jesus says, 'You will see heaven opened and angels of light ascending and descending upon the Son of Man.'[41] The term 'Son of Man', as we have noted, is not a title that separates Christ from the rest of humanity. Rather, it points to Christ's representation of true humanity. He expresses our deepest and most original identity, made in the image and likeness of God.

Jacob had experienced the glory of God in a place. In the New Testament tradition, the glory of God is made manifest in a person. Jesus embodies the glory of the One who is the Self within all selves. He reveals the light that enlightens every person. 'And the Word became flesh,' as St John writes, 'and lived among us, and we have seen his glory.'[42]

He is the perfect expression of the Word that has uttered all life into being. St Paul says, 'in him the whole fullness of deity dwells bodily'.[43] The fullness of God's glory shines forth in a body. It is the perception of this truth that leads someone like George MacLeod to say that 'matter matters'. Shining through the material world is the spiritual world that upholds it and enlivens it. Christ reveals to us what is at the heart of matter. Hidden in the mystery of our own bodies and the body of all creation is 'the unseeable One glory of the everlasting world'.

St Paul describes Christ as 'the Lord of glory' who was 'crucified' by the world.[44] Just as the glory that is in creation is driven down and desecrated, so the One who perfectly reflects glory is rejected and nailed to a tree. In St John's description of the death of Jesus, the evangelist draws our attention to the practice of execution common in the Roman Empire in which the legs of criminals were broken to speed their death by crucifixion. 'When they came to Jesus', he says, 'they did not break his legs.'[45] St John is pointing to the rootedness of Jesus in the eternity and glory that are the pillars of his being. Even when Jesus himself is led to doubt the presence of God in the midst of his suffering, the pillars of his inner being remain firm.

The sixteenth-century Protestant reformer, Martin Luther, stressed again and again that it is in the shame of the cross that we are shown the depths of the hiddenness of God's glory. The glory and eternity that Christ bears witness to in his life are concealed at the point of his suffering. In his anguish he cries out in the words of Psalm 22, 'My God, my God, why have you forsaken me?' The pillars of life's temple are everlasting, but in Christ's crucifixion, as in the deaths and sufferings of people in every age and in every place, the everlasting pillars are not seen.

The Eternity of the Self

St Paul says that 'our lives are hidden with Christ in God'.[46] Part of the hiddenness that we experience is the concealment of glory and eternity in the midst of the struggles and pain of life. We long for liberation, not only for ourselves and people throughout the world but for the whole of creation in its cries of anguish and death. St Paul expresses this hope when he prays 'that creation itself will be set free from its bondage to decay and obtain the freedom of the glory of the children of God'.[47]

Grace is given that we may glimpse the hidden foundations of life and turn to them, even when they seem most obscured by the wrongs of life. Repentance is a turning away from everything that denies the light and the eternity in which life is rooted. It is a returning to a reverence for the glory that is in each one of us and in all that has been born of the mystery of God.

The Book of Wisdom says that 'God has made us in the image of his own eternity'.[48] We have been made 'not out of nothing . . . but out of God's own endless glory', as George MacDonald says.[49] The essence of the mystery of our being and of all being is everlasting. In 'The Marriage of Heaven and Hell' William Blake refers to the ancient belief that the world will be consumed by fire at the end of time. The angel of Genesis 3, who protects with a flaming sword the east gate of Eden, will be commanded, says Blake, 'to leave his guard at the tree of life, and when he does, the whole of creation will be consumed, and appear infinite, and holy whereas it now appears finite and corrupt'.[50] Death's powers of stripping away all that is impermanent will reveal the deeper truth of life's everlasting pillars.

Jesus speaks of dying in order to live, of losing life in order to find it.[51] His words point not only to the final moment of physical death but to a way of living in every moment. They speak of our need forever to be dying to the little self, the false and destructive self of our ego, in order to be alive to the true Self in whom our life is everlasting.

Gerard Manley Hopkins says that we are like 'immortal diamond'.[52] The fire of death will not destroy us. Rather, it will reveal the brilliance of life that cannot be undone. In 'That Nature is a Heraclitean Fire' Hopkins sees resurrection as the 'heart's-clarion' which wakes us to what is deepest. It is in the context of losing everything through the fire of death that we find our most precious depths. We discover that we are 'what Christ is', says Hopkins, 'immortal diamond'.

But for Hopkins, to become 'what Christ is' is not to become something other than himself. Rather, it is to become truly himself by dying to the falseness of what he has become. As Hopkins says elsewhere, 'each mortal thing' has been created to do 'one thing', to be 'itself'. In his poem 'As kingfishers catch fire', he says that the cry of every creature is, '*What I do is me: for that I came.*'[53] It is the cry of the bird in the air and the flower of the field, just as it is the deepest cry emerging from the soul of every human being. The glory of God is truly shown in our lives to the degree that we are most radically ourselves.

But how have we built on these foundations of glory? St Paul envisages the judgement of the last day as a disclosure of whether or not we have become truly ourselves. The truth 'will be revealed with fire', he says. The works of 'gold', as he calls them, that have been built into the glory of our foundations will endure. The works of 'straw', on the other hand, that bear no relation to the true depths of our being will be burned up. His vision is that the heart of who we are will be saved, 'but only as through fire'.[54]

The Eternity of the Self

In the biblical tradition judgement is given to set things right, not to dwell forever on what has gone wrong. Nelson Mandela, the former President of South Africa, who as much as any other human being might have been justified in focusing on the failure of the human spirit, calls us to the strength and the glory that are deeper than our failures. In his historic inaugural address he quoted the following words:

Our deepest fear is not that we are inadequate.
Our deepest fear is that we are powerful beyond measure.
It is our light, not our darkness, that most frightens us.
We ask ourselves, who am I to be brilliant, gorgeous,
    talented and fabulous?
Actually, who are you *not* to be?
You are a child of God.
Your playing small doesn't serve the world.
There is nothing enlightened about shrinking so that
    other people won't feel insecure around you.
We are born to make manifest the glory of God that is
    within us.
It's not just in some of us; it's in everyone.
And as we let our own light shine, we unconsciously
    give other people permission to do the same.
As we are liberated from our own fear,
our presence automatically liberates others.[55]

Edwin Muir, in his poem 'The Transfiguration', sees healing as something that issues up from a glory that is deep within us and within all things, 'from the ground' as he says.[56] The grace of transfiguration enables those who have done terrible wrong, 'the lurkers under doorways' as he calls them, to come out of themselves. It frees those who have hidden under the inglorious failures of their lives to step out of their 'dungeons'. The agony of wrong, he says, will be 'undone'. Even the cross will be 'dismantled' and 'the tormented wood' that has been used for crucifixion instead will 'grow into a tree in a green springing corner of young Eden'. 'Eden', our place of deepest and truest origin, is forever 'young'. Our roots of glory and eternity still shoot forth.

As the Prophecy of Isaiah says, 'let the earth open that salvation may spring up'.[57] Let the ground of our being open to reveal the glory that has been planted within us. The Jewish mystics liked to refer to the words of a divine promise, 'Open for me an opening like the point of a needle, and I will open for you gates like the gates of the Sanctuary.'[58] In opening even a pinprick of the true depths of our inner being we glimpse a glory that is unbounded.

Words for Meditation

'You made me in the image of your own eternity' *(Wisdom 2:23).*

7

THE PRESENCE OF THE SELF

The feet of the human body represent presence. They are associated with being rooted firmly on the ground. The feet are identified also with movement. Where is it that we have chosen to place ourselves in our lives, and what does it mean to be a person of presence?

The Prophecy of Ezekiel envisages the temple filled with cloud. It is the cloud of the mystery of God's presence. From the cloud the prophet hears the words, 'This is the place for the soles of my feet, where I will reside forever.'[1] The temple represents the place of God's eternal presence, yet Solomon's Temple was a passing temple. Likewise the temple of creation and the temple of our human bodies are passing. There will be a time when they are no more. Ezekiel's vision is pointing to the everlasting presence of God in 'the temple not made with hands', as the Scriptures say.[2] The place of God's eternal dwelling is the sanctuary of our inner beings. God resides forever at the heart of our life and of all life.

In the Old Testament, as well as in the New, the divine presence is seen both as transcendent and immanent. God is forever beyond us and more than anything that we can conceive of. In that sense God is wholly other. God is also deep within the mystery of creation, closer to us than our very breathing. In that sense God is with us, and indeed

more present to us than we are to ourselves. The Prophecy
of Isaiah says to the people of Israel that God is their
'Maker' as well as their 'Husband'.[3] God has created them
and is other than them. At the same time God is one flesh
with them, wedded to the mystery of their beings.

In the New Testament tradition Jesus is the embodiment
of God's presence. At his birth he is associated with the
name 'Immanuel', which means 'God with us'.[4] Throughout his life he describes himself as 'one with the Father' and
thus as carrying the presence of God.[5] In his resurrection
appearance to the two Marys, St Matthew says that they
'took hold of his feet, and worshipped him'.[6] They cherish
his presence. The one who died is with them, and in love
they cleave to him.

We know what it is like to be separated from one whom
we love. We long to be with them, to see the sparkle of life
in their eyes and to smell the scent of their skin. We yearn
to hold them and be touched by their presence. The modern
artist Doris Salcedo of Colombia explores themes of presence in relation to the 'disappeared' of her country. Those
who have been abducted and killed by politically motivated
death squads are represented in her works by abandoned
homes and by empty shoes. People's shoes are very personal
to them. Usually they are worn by no one else. The image
of the empty shoe speaks powerfully of absence. It can
evoke the painful desire to see again or to hold again the
one who is no longer present.[7]

The Gospel writers reflect on the feet of the human form
as a symbol of presence. Just as in St Matthew's Gospel,
Mary Magdalene 'took hold of Jesus' feet and worshipped
him', so in St John's Gospel, Mary of Bethany 'took a
pound of costly perfume made of pure nard, anointed
Jesus' feet, and wiped them with her hair'.[8] It is a sensuous

image of delighting in the presence of the other. St John says that Mary's house was 'filled with the fragrance of the perfume'. Jesus' presence to her was like a fragrance that filled her being.

The parallel in St Luke's Gospel is of 'a woman in the city, who was a sinner', says Luke.[9] She comes to Jesus while he is at table eating in a Pharisee's house. In Jesus' presence she weeps and begins 'to bathe his feet with her tears and to dry them with her hair'. The Pharisee is critical of Jesus for allowing 'a sinner' to touch him. Yet Jesus says that she has expressed such love for him because she has experienced forgiveness. His presence has evoked tears in her. His love has released from her depths the desire to change. It is a desire deep within the human heart. In the depths of our beings we long to be true and to be set free from falseness. It is the presence of love that releases us to be true to these depths.

In St John's Gospel, Judas objects to the anointing of Jesus' feet. 'Why was this perfume not sold for three hundred denarii,' he asks, 'and the money given to the poor?' Judas is the one who will betray Jesus. Nevertheless his question needs to be answered. In one way or another it is a question that occurs to all of us. What is the relationship between presence and justice? How, like Mary, do we give ourselves to celebrating the presence of God, including the sacredness of the people whom we love, and at the same time care for the poor?

In what appears to be a revision to St John's Gospel, the following words are added: 'Judas said this not because he cared about the poor, but because he was a thief; he kept the common purse and used to steal what was put into it.'[10] Whether Judas was a thief or not, his question still raises important issues. The problem with the way he puts the question is that it suggests that either we can be extravagant or compassionate, but not both. Either we lavishly delight in another person's presence or we give ourselves to working for justice. But is this not a false tension? What sort of justice results if it is not grounded in a belief in the pricelessness of each human presence? Does it not result in the sort of parody of egalitarianism that we have witnessed in political systems in our world when equality for all is claimed without at the same time calling for a reverence for each person? And is a willingness to let go extravagantly not related also to a willingness to let go to the spirit of justice? As the Prophecy of Amos says, 'Let justice roll down like waters, and righteousness like an everflowing stream.'[11] There is nothing restrained about the passion for justice. It is like the passion of love.

In the biblical tradition the presence of God, the coming of God, is linked inextricably with justice. 'God is coming to judge the earth,' says the Psalmist.[12] God is coming to establish 'justice' and 'equity'.[13] For the prophets, the presence of God, or the presence of God's messenger, is equated with a setting of things right and a restoring of harmony. 'How beautiful upon the mountains are the feet of the messenger who announces peace.'[14]

Mary's song at the conception of the Christ-child celebrates God as coming to establish justice, 'to bring down the powerful from their thrones and to lift up the lowly'.[15] The disclosing of the divine presence is for the establishing of what is just. Any attempt to create a polarity between justice, on the one hand, and the celebration of presence, on the other, is a false contrast. It is precisely as we come to know the preciousness of human presence that we work most passionately for what is just.

As we have seen all along in exploring the emanations of

God's mystery in the human form, each emanation is linked inseparably to the others. The might of the left arm and of justice needs always to be rooted by feet planted firmly on the ground. The vital energies of the genitals and of creativity need to be protected and inspired by the strength of our right arm and by love. Our desires of the heart and yearnings for beauty need to be in harmony with our faculties of thought and gifts of wisdom. There is a flow between all of the emanations. None of them is to be isolated. As St Paul says, 'the body is one'.[16] Just as we seek unity between ourselves collectively, so we are to seek unity within ourselves. We need to ask if we are alive to the whole of our beings. Are we allowing the different dimensions of the mystery of God's image within us to be awakened?

I have many memories of Central American refugees flooding into Canada in the mid-1980s. Many of these men and women had lost everything, family, friends, possessions, and the right to live in their home countries. Some of them now were working for political change in Canada and for the welcoming of other refugees. My memories are twofold. One is of their passion for justice. The other is of their capacity for partying, extravagantly! These were people who knew the preciousness of presence and the gift of the moment. In large part this was because they knew what it was to lose presence, in many cases the presence of the ones whom they most cherished. Their parties could have been described as 'over-the-top', like the costly perfume spilled out on Jesus' feet. Someone might have asked, 'Why was all this wine and food not sold and the money given to other refugees?' It is a question that each of us needs to ask repeatedly in our lives. My guess, however, is that for most of us much of the time the answer lies not in giving ourselves less to partying but more to justice. The answer lies in the realm of learning to give ourselves to the celebration of presence in such a way that our desire for justice is further fed in our lives.

The coming of God is associated with justice, with a clearing away of what is wrong. It is a clearing away of wrong, however, in order to make room for the presence of love. Love is at the heart of the divine presence. The Prophecy of Isaiah says, 'The mountains may depart and the hills be removed, but my steadfast love shall not depart from you.'[17] The eternal presence is a fire of love. It is passionate like that of the beloved's in the Song of Songs. 'Its flames are flashes of fire, a raging flame.'[18] At its heart is the desire for the other's presence. 'Let me see your face,' says the beloved, 'let me hear your voice; for your voice is sweet, and your face is lovely.'[19] The mystery of God is one of passionate presence. You shall not be called 'Forsaken', says Isaiah, 'for the Lord delights in you'.[20] God is ever present, longing for us also to be present.

In speaking of the 'coming' of God, sometimes the impression is created that God is somehow 'absent'. Rather, it is we who are absent. God is totally present. As the twentieth-century teacher Henri Nouwen used to say, 'We all have a home address, but we can't often be found there.' We live in a type of exile from our place of deepest origin and identity. St Augustine, in reflecting on the spiritual journey of his life, and in particular on the years of separation from God, says that it was not that God had been separated from him but that he had been separated from himself. As he writes in his *Confessions*, 'You were within me, and I was in the world outside myself . . . You were with me, but I was not with you.'[21]

The Prophecy of Isaiah says, 'Why did no one answer

when I called?'[22] Is it not, as Nouwen says, because in fact we are not there. We live in a state of distraction most of the time rather than in a state of presence. We chase the future, the next ambition and the next idea, and end up missing the moment. Isaiah says that God is calling out, 'Here I am, here I am.'[23] From the heart of our being and from the heart of every moment, God is saying 'Return to me'.[24] It is a return to our home address and to the present moment.

This is not to say that God is somehow limited to the present, and is not also ahead of us in the ever-new moment that is unfolding. As William Blake says, God 'before, behind, above, beneath, around'.[25] There is no time and no place where God is not present. In every place and in every moment we can be alert to the One who is eternally Now. Every second of our lives is a new gift, never given to us before. In every person we meet and in every experience of our lives God desires our presence. We are being called into an awareness of the present moment. It is now that God is seeking us.

Our tendency to miss the One who is Now, the One who is ever present to us with longing, is paralleled by our religious tendency to look away from the immediate and the ordinary to the so-called 'holy' places and 'holy' times. Jesus resisted such a division. He criticised those who had opposed King David's action when he and his men, fatigued and hungry, 'entered the house of God and took and ate the bread of the Presence'.[26] The holy presence of God cannot be confined by religious boundaries of time and space. The 'bread of the Presence', like the blessed bread of the sacrament, is holy, but it is holy not in an exclusive sense. It is pointing us to the holiness of all bread and all wine. The holy Presence is in every particle of matter and in the entire expanse of the universe. The answer to religion's tendency to divide the 'holy' from the 'ordinary' is not to try to strip our religious sites and gatherings of a sense of the sacred. The answer lies in recovering our sense of the sacredness of every moment of life. It is not to make the holy ordinary but to see that the ordinary is holy.

Jesus represented a breaking open of religious boundaries in order to declare the whole of life and every person sacred. At the moment of his death, says St Matthew, 'the curtain in the temple was torn in two, from top to bottom'.[27] The inner sanctum of the temple, the 'Holy of Holies' as it was known, is everywhere present. It cannot be contained or monopolised by religious customs and claims. As St John says, in speaking of the Word through whom all things have been expressed into being, 'He was in the world, and the world came into being through him; yet the world did not know him.'[28] Jesus comes to make known the One who is totally present to us but from whom we have become absent, the One who knows us better than we know ourselves but whom we have forgotten. The presence of God in every moment of life is not something that we achieve. It is pure gift. We can only receive it, but we do need to open our eyes to the Presence. No one else can do this for us.

In the cloud of unknowing Ezekiel sees four living creatures who embody the mystery of God's presence in creation.[29] On the earth beside each living creature is a wheel. It gleams like emerald. The construction of the wheel is like a wheel within a wheel. It can move in all four directions. It is a picture of omnipresence, of being present in all directions. The rims of the wheels, and even the spokes, are 'full of eyes all around'. The spirit, says Ezekiel, is 'in the wheels'. Like the feet of the human form they represent the place of presence, the place of touching the earth. It is a presence alive with consciousness, 'full of eyes'. It is into this type of awareness that we are being invited, to be awakened into a fuller consciousness.

In the Jewish mystical tradition, the presence of God often is seen in feminine terms. It is known as the 'Shekinah', and is associated especially with images of the earth, the moon and the night. This suggests a deep and intuitive knowing of the Presence rather than simply an outward and intellectual type of knowing. Similarly, the Sabbath, the special day of God's presence, also came to be viewed in feminine terms. It is referred to as the 'Matrona', the Mother or Bride. She is portrayed as pregnant with the presence of God. The Sabbath is full of the holy emanations of the divine. Mystery and wisdom, strength and beauty, creativity and glory all are born to us through the day of rest. On the Sabbath God is celebrated as the One who is present.

What does it mean to be made in the image of God, to be made in the image of the One who is wholly present? Deep in our forgotten self is a capacity to be fully present to the moment and to one another, to be awake and aware rather than half-sleepwalking in our lives.

We sometimes speak of a person having 'presence'. What do we mean? It is a phrase that is hard to define. One of the things that we mean, at the risk of stating the obvious, is that a person with presence is very present. Such a person conveys presence without necessarily having to display it in actions and words. It is not so much what the person says or does. It relates more to the way the person is alert and alive to the moment, conscious of the mystery of life and of the interrelatedness of all things.

In the Gospel story of Jesus visiting the home of Mary

and Martha in Bethany, Mary is described as sitting at Jesus' feet, listening to him. Martha, on the other hand, is rushing about, doing the important and necessary things of preparing food and providing hospitality. Martha complains about Mary not helping, to which Jesus responds, 'Martha, Martha, you are worried and distracted by many things; there is need of only one thing. Mary has chosen the better part, which will not be taken away from her.'[30]

The point, of course, is not that we are all to sit about doing nothing. Rather, the point is that Mary sitting at Jesus' feet, listening, is an image of presence. Times of still-ness and meditation can be moments of great awareness. At such moments we can be alert to the gift of the moment and to the One who is present in every moment. The chal-lenge is to practise presence in everything that we do, to bring an inner attentiveness into the busy as well as the quiet times of our lives. The invitation is to be free from distraction in whatever we happen to be doing. It is to be present to one another and to the mystery at the heart of every second of life. The great disciplines of silence and contemplation in our spiritual inheritance are designed to exercise our inner faculties of awareness, so that when we return to engage in the details of family life and work we do so with a sharpened sense of the sacredness of the present.

To be a person of presence is to be alert to the mystery of who we are. It is to be attentive to the wisdom that has been woven into our beings, to be awake to the strength that we have been endowed with. It is to be alive to the beauty that is at the heart of life, to be aware of our capacity for new beginnings. It is to be present to the glory in which our life and all life is eternally rooted.

In Jewish tradition, the Sabbath is the day of presence. In the Genesis account it is on the seventh day that God finishes the work of creation.[31] Without the seventh day creation is not complete. Stillness and restfulness are essential to creation's ongoing life and wellbeing. In Jewish religious practice, on the Sabbath eve, when work ceases, the candles are lit. Just as creation begins with the words, 'Let there be light', so the day of presence begins with kindling the lights. It recalls the light that is at the beginning and heart of creation. The day of presence is about being reconnected to the heart of life. It is a day of consciously seeking the presence of God, as well as being aware of one another's presence. The Jewish practice of presence, like the different practices of stillness in our various religious traditions, is about being renewed at our deepest level of self-identity. The focus is not on what we do but on who we are. It is the freedom of simply being ourselves rather than having to achieve or perform through our work and our actions.

The Book of Exodus speaks about 'sanctifying' the Sabbath.[32] In Hebrew the same word is used for a man and woman betrothing themselves to each other. The emphasis is on becoming one with the day of presence. The seventh day is not regarded as an appendage to creation. It is not simply stuck on at the end. Rather, it is the climax of creation, the completion or consummation. The six days of work lead to the seventh day of being. The Sabbath, therefore, is viewed as an experience of eternity. Our work will pass. Our important roles all will be taken away from us, but the heart of our being, made in the image of God, is our 'I amness'. It is this that is celebrated on the day of presence. In Jewish tradition, just as one longs for the Sabbath all the days of the week, so one longs for the eternal Sabbath all the days of one's life. It is about longing to be truly ourselves, to be fully present to our own depths and to the unique mystery of one another's depths.

Aspects of the Jewish Sabbath have been transferred into Christian practice. Instead of Saturday, however, it is Sunday, the first day of the week, that is observed by many Christians as the day of rest. In the early Church, of course, Sunday, the day of Christ's resurrection, was seen as coming out of the Sabbath. This made a profound link between stillness and new life, or between the deep sleep of death, on the one hand, and the waking up to resurrection, on the other. Unless we give ourselves over to times of restfulness and letting go, we will not truly be awake to life, or, as Jesus taught, unless we die we will not truly live. In both Jewish and Christian practice, however, Sabbath observance has tended towards religious legalism. Many of us who grew up in sabbatarian traditions will remember this not as a liberating practice but as a stultifying one. For many it was a day of inhibition and restraint, instead of being a day of freedom from work and therefore of liberty to play and to delight in one another's presence.

I remember seeing a Zen Buddhist doing a walking meditation. Each footstep spoke of sensitivity to the ground and of awareness. It was an image of presence. In the Old Testament tradition, Moses at the burning bush is told to take off his sandals for the place on which he is standing is holy ground.[33] In all of the great mystical traditions, the whole of the earth is holy and every place in which we encounter others is holy ground, to be walked on with awareness and reverence.

Something of this capacity to give ourselves to the moment is naturally present in a child. We all will have memories of dangling our feet into water as children, or playing in puddles with a complete forgetfulness that there might be anything else to do that day. The capacity to be captured by the moment and filled with wonder is a gift of childhood and of childlikeness. 'To such as these,' says Jesus, 'the kingdom of God belongs.'[34]

One of the marks of the kingdom of God in its utter simplicity is knowing the singularity of each moment. Every moment is a new arrival, a new bestowal from God. Abraham Heschel says that 'the cardinal sin is in our failure not to sense the grandeur of the moment, the marvel and mystery of being'.[35]

I met a Jewish man in New Jersey on one occasion, who in fact had become a Christian. He told me about one of the most important moments in his life. He was a young boy at a Jewish summer camp. Word got around that the Rebbe, the revered leader of their Hasidic community, was down the river and was waiting for the boys. When they found him he was standing in the water praying, rocking back and forth in the Hasidic style of prayer. The Rebbe said only one thing to them, 'The water that we now see passing us will never flow past us again.' They then joined him in his meditation, standing in the river rocking back and forth together in silence. The young boy was immediately next to the Rebbe. The rhythmic motion of prayer and the steady flow of the river put him to sleep. When he woke up, all of the other boys were away and he was being held up by the arm of the Rebbe, still rocking in prayer. The Rebbe said nothing to him, but looked into his eyes and smiled.

I asked the man why he had become a Christian. He said, 'Because I found in Christ what that Rebbe had taught me to see. I found in Christ the One who is totally present.' As Jesus says in St Matthew's Gospel, 'Remember, I am with you always, even to the end of the age.'[36]

The Jewish mystics have taught a living entirely in the present moment as the heart of spiritual awareness. The form of meditative discipline that was developed by the kabbalists in the Middle Ages was called 'one-pointed concentration'.[37] It was a focusing on the moment, and on God as the heart of every moment. This practice was known as 'cleaving' to God. It was a meditative practice that involved not a stepping aside from the details of daily life but being aware of God's presence in the midst of the everyday details of life. In every creature, in every human being, in every created thing God is present. Seeking God, therefore, is not about searching for One who is somehow absent, for there is nothing in which God cannot be found. God is the Life of the world. It is not away from life that we are to look for the Mystery but deep within it, deeper than the distortions and falseness that have covered the holy Presence.

To practise the presence of God is to be free to live in the moment. It is to be liberated from the way in which the past and the future can encroach upon us and hold us in a type of bondage to the fears and preoccupations of yesterday and tomorrow. 'Do not worry about tomorrow,' says Jesus, 'for tomorrow will bring worries of its own.'[38] At the most important moments of life, at moments of creativity and lovemaking or in painful moments of parting and loss, we need to have a type of forgetfulness of the past and the future in order to be present to the wonder and mystery of what is happening, as well as to the struggles and challenges of the moment. Perhaps it is particularly at painful moments that we prefer to look away from the present in the hope of denying suffering. The promise of God's presence, however, is that it is deeper even than the struggles of death.

The Psalmist frequently calls on God for help so that his feet will not slip. 'Save me, O God, for the waters come up to my neck. I sink in deep mire, where there is no foothold.'[39] It is especially when we are challenged by chaos in our lives, or threatened by what disturbs and upsets us, that we are liable to lose the grace of presence and begin to flounder. Presence is about oneness with life. It is about oneness with the One who is the Presence of life itself, and who holds us even when all else is unsure.

In the New Testament Jesus is described by St John as washing the feet of the disciples.[40] It is a washing of the place of presence. It is a cleansing of what obscures a true sensitivity and awareness in the disciples. Especially, it is a freeing them to be more fully alive to Christ's love. To be restored in our sense of presence is to be set free in relation to all of the emanations of God's light. To be a person of presence is to be awake to the need for justice and beauty. It is to be attentive to wisdom and the possibilities for new conception and birth. Above all else it is to be alive to love.

As well as washing the feet of the disciples, Jesus teaches them to wash one another's feet. He teaches them how to set free awareness in one another, and how to be a presence of love. In the washing of their feet he shows them the way of love, which is to serve, just as he had taught them the way of strength, which is to forgive. Forgive one another, he says, 'not seven times, but seventy times seven times.'[41] When we fail to forgive we make it impossible to be present to the other. The one whom we hate will receive only the smallest part of our being, and, what is more, it is a false part. As Edwin Muir says, it is 'unnatural' not to forgive.[42] It has no root in our deepest place of origin. It has no place in eternity, for we are made to be present to one another. We are made to be part of one another.

The grace of true presence is something that we can help restore and heal in one another through love and forgiveness. We become truly ourselves not in isolation but in relationship, through the giving and receiving of presence, including, of course, the giving and receiving of presents!

In the story of the forgiving father in St Luke's Gospel, the prodigal son, who has wasted his inheritance and been false to his father as well as to himself, comes to a turning point in his life.[43] Jesus' way of putting it is to say that 'when he came to himself' he knew what he was to do. Repentance or turning around, as we have seen, is about returning to our truest identity. The prodigal son in coming to himself knows where his healing lies. He says, 'I will get up and go to my father.' His reconciliation with his father is his reconciliation also with himself. 'While he was still far off,' says Jesus, 'his father saw him and was filled with compassion; he ran and put his arms around him and kissed him.' We belong to one another. Our wholeness is found in the reconciliation of relationship. The father says, 'This son of mine was dead and is alive again; he was lost and is found.'

How are we to be found again? Abraham Heschel says that 'existence is co-existence'.[44] Relationship is deep in the mystery of creation. In the Christian tradition, God is revealed as Trinity. At the heart of the mystery of life is God, not in isolated individuality but in relationship. Being in communion is the very essence of God. As Thomas Aquinas in the thirteenth century said, 'in God relation and essence do not differ from each other, but are one and the same'.[45] In other words, it is not that God enters communion but that God is communion, or as St John says, 'God is love'.[46] Our forgotten self, made in the image of God, will be recovered not simply on our own but in the mutuality of giving and receiving in love.

The Song of Songs, perhaps the most beautiful love

poem in our Jewish-Christian inheritance, expresses this in terms of the coming together of the beloved and the lover. It is a meeting in love, a marriage of presences. True presence is never simply about either giving or receiving. It is about desiring to give and to receive. This is as true for intimate sexual relationship as it is for the great collective relationships of our world, between north and south or between rich and poor or male and female. As Abraham Heschel says, 'I become a person by knowing the meaning of receiving and giving. I become a person when I begin to reciprocate.'[47]

The movement in the Song of Songs begins with the beloved coming to the lover and saying, 'Arise, my love, my fair one, and come away.'[48] The invitation is to join him, to come out of herself to him and to move with him in relationship. He knocks at her door, says the Song of Songs, and, although she desires him, she delays, 'I had put off my garment; how could I put it on again? I had bathed my feet; how could I soil them?'[49]

What is it that makes us delay in giving ourselves passionately to relationship, or in sharing our presence fully with others? Is it, like the lover, that we are concerned about keeping our 'feet' clean? Are we torn between the desire to open our presence to others and the fear of the messiness of doing so? Passion for justice, like passion for love or creativity, is not tidy. Who knows what will happen when we begin to expose the powerful energies of our presence?

The lover delays and for the time being misses the moment. She loses the beloved and cannot find him. 'I sought him,' she says, 'but did not find him; I called him, but he gave no answer.'[50] Her words express the frustration of not having responded when she should have. In her heart she had desired him, but in apprehension she had held back. She was certain of her passion, but she had failed to act on it. What are the desires of our hearts that we have suppressed, and ended up missing the moment? Who are the people with whom we wanted to share ourselves and gifts, and instead we withdrew?

Like the prodigal son, the lover finally comes to herself and knows what she is to do. She finds the beloved and says to him, 'Come, my beloved, let us go forth into the fields, and lodge in the villages; let us go out early to the vineyards, and see whether the vines have budded, whether the grape blossoms have opened and the pomegranates are in bloom. There I will give you my love.'[51] We find what has been lost in ourselves by giving ourselves away, in love.

In the kabbalistic community of Safed on the shores of the Sea of Galilee, it was the custom of husbands and wives to make love at midnight on the Sabbath. The belief was that the longing for sexual union reflected the deeper longing that is in us for union with God. The joy of restfulness on the Sabbath was likened to the deep physical restfulness that follows the passion of lovemaking. Sabbath was not only a day that fed the hunger of the soul. It fed also the God-given desires of the body. It was a day of food and drink, of comfort and pleasure. As one of the rabbi's said, 'Sleeping on Shabbat is a joy.'[52]

In all of this there is a confidence in the deepest hungers in the human soul and body, the yearning for union between us and the desire for union with God. This is not to deny that our desires become terribly distorted. Have we not all experienced being taken over at times by a confusion of longings? But do we not also know that there is a difference between healthy desire and unhealthy desire? Why then, as William Blake asks, have our religious traditions tended to call the deep physical and sexual desires of humanity a 'Crime'?[53] Why is it that we cannot be freed to see them rather as manifestations of the deepest desire that God has planted in us, the desire for the Beloved, the longing for the One who is Love. Then, when we make our mistakes, we can be encouraged by one another to change our lives on the basis of believing that it is not our deepest desires that are wrong. Rather, it is our failure to know what will truly satisfy these desires.

God has placed a holiness of desire within us. We are being invited to get in touch with that desire, to 'drink from the river of God's delights' as the Psalmist says.[54] God is present in all things and in every moment longing for us in love. As Martin Buber says, 'You know always in your heart that you need God more than everything; but do you know too that God needs you?'[55] The true voice of the soul, as the Psalmist expresses it, is the response to God's longing, 'as the deer longs for flowing streams, so my soul longs for you, O God'.[56]

In Jewish tradition the day of presence is viewed in feminine terms, as Bride or Queen. The medieval Jewish mystics of Safed were known for actually going out into the fields to meet the coming Presence on the Sabbath eve, and reciting the love poems of the Song of Songs. Eventually this practice deteriorated into simply going out into the courtyard of the synagogue to greet the Sabbath, and then finally into the current practice of the door of the synagogue being opened and merely bowing to the west to greet the approaching Bride. For many of us this is perhaps a metaphor of how we find it easier to bow to the idea of God's presence in all things than actually taking our bodies and energies out to the people and places of our world where God is longing for our presence.

In the Gospels, Jesus says to his hearers, 'Follow me'.[57] The One who is totally present to us is forever inviting us to step further into the holy Presence. As Edwin Muir writes in his poem 'The Return', the re-entering of the place of our deepest belonging is never about going back to something in our past. It is about taking 'the road that always, early or late, runs on before'.[58]

The holy Presence is eternally opening immediately before us. It is not God who is absent from us. Rather, we are absent from God at the heart of life. It is not Christ who needs to come again. It is we who need to come back to ourselves and to the present moment where Christ is forever with us. The Psalmist says, 'Seek God's presence continually.'[59] The invitation is to be alive to the holy Presence in every moment and in every person we meet.

Words for Meditation

'My soul longs for you, O God' *(Psalm 42:1).*

Appendix
A Way of Awareness

The Jewish mystics emphasised an awareness of God in the midst of life, of being alert to the One who is Now and at the heart of every moment. Awareness of the Holy Presence was nurtured by disciplines of prayer and meditation. This was not to suggest that God was more present in 'religious' moments than in 'ordinary' moments. Through spiritual disciplines the inner faculties of perception were sharpened so that in the whole of life there could be a clearer sense of the presence of God.

One of the keys to this way of awareness was called 'one-pointed concentration'. It was applied in the midst of the daily details of life as a way of being present to the sacredness of each moment. It was applied also to the discipline of meditation. During times of silent prayer 'one-pointed concentration' was a way of focusing in prayer on the various parts of the body. Just as it can be helpful to go to holy places to pray, so in this tradition the human body is a temple. Just as outwardly we move from one part of a sacred site to another, into the side chapels of a cathedral or to the crossing at its heart, so in prayer we can visit the different parts of the temple of our body.

In Jewish practice the crown of the head, associated with mystery, is always the place to begin in meditation. It reminds us of the mystery of our being, and of our own being linked inseparably to the Mystery of God's Being. From the crown of the head we then can move through the entire body, to the centre of our forehead, to our right arm and left arm, to our heart, to our genitals, to our right leg and left leg, and to the soles of our feet. The intention simply is to be prayerfully attentive, and to allow our awareness of the mystery of our body, made in the image of God, to recall us to our true selves. Our breathing can provide the rhythm for this inner movement. In our upward movement of breathing in we can focus on the crown of the head. Then, in our downward movement of breathing out we can focus on the different parts of the body, one at a time, always returning to the crown of the head in our intake of breath. When we focus on our forehead, for instance, or on any other part of our body, we can allow this to express our desire to be renewed in wisdom, or in the other emanations of God's image within us.

In Jewish tradition the sacred name of God, YHWH, was incorporated in the practice of meditation. In focusing on the heart, a kabbalist would also envisage the letters of God's name within him, almost as if they were inscribed into his heart. The same was true in focusing on any other part of the body. The understanding was that all of the emanations of God were included in the one sacred name. In adapting this form of meditation for use today, words may or may not be helpful. At the end of each chapter, however, I have suggested phrases that can be included. In focusing on the heart, for instance, the words 'Strength and beauty are in your sanctuary' can be silently repeated as a way of being recalled to our true strength and beauty. The repetition of words can help focus our inner attention.

The kabbalists referred to meditation as 'choosing life'. It is not about stepping away from life but about returning to the One who is the source of life. It is not about denying the vitality of our bodies but about becoming more alive in the whole of our beings. As one Jewish mystic put it, meditation is like being 'bound in the bundle of life'. It is a re-binding of ourselves to the goodness of Life.

NOTES

Introduction

1. Genesis 1:26.
2. D. Erdman (ed.), 'The Marriage of Heaven and Hell', in *The Complete Poetry and Prose of William Blake* (Anchor Books, 1988), p. 34.
3. John Scotus Eriugena, *Periphyseon (The Division of Nature)* (Bellarmin, 1987), p. 587.
4. *Periphyseon*, p. 191.
5. Genesis 4:7.
6. Hebrews 11:3.
7. Galatians 3:22.
8. Romans 7:20.
9. Romans 8:4.
10. E. Muir, 'One Foot in Eden', in *Collected Poems* (Faber, 1984), p. 227.
11. 'Jerusalem', in *The Complete Poetry and Prose of William Blake*, pp. 223, 156.
12. 'Jerusalem', in *The Complete Poetry and Prose of William Blake*, p. 193.
13. B. Bokser (trans.), *Abraham Isaac Kook* (Paulist, 1978), p. 63.
14. See J. P. Newell, *The Book of Creation* (Canterbury Press, 1999).
15. John 1:1,3.
16. 'The Divine Image', in *The Complete Poetry and Prose of William Blake*, p. 13.
17. Ezekiel 1:1.
18. Ezekiel 1:28.
19. 'The Incarnate One', in *Collected Poems*, p. 228.
20. A. Heschel, *Who is Man?* (Stanford University Press, 1965), p. 49.

Notes

1 The Mystery of the Self

1. 'Jerusalem', in *The Complete Poetry and Prose of William Blake*, p. 158.
2. M. Buber (ed.), *Ecstatic Confessions: The Heart of Mysticism* (Syracuse University Press, 1996), p. 156.
3. Acts 17:28.
4. Ezekiel 1:28.
5. 1 Timothy 6:16.
6. *Abraham Isaac Kook*, p. 261.
7. This point has been well made by many of today's feminist writers. See, for example, E. Johnson, *She Who Is: The Mystery of God in Feminist Theological Discourse* (Crossroad, 1997).
8. Genesis 1:27.
9. Exodus 3:14.
10. M. Buber, *I and Thou* (T. & T. Clark, 1970).
11. *Ecstatic Confessions*, p 1.
12. D. Matt (ed.), *The Essential Kabbalah* (Harper San Francisco, 1996), p. 153.
13. *I and Thou*, p. 64.
14. *I and Thou*, p. 65.
15. Psalm 139:13–14.
16. *Who is Man?*, p. 37.
17. *Who is Man?*, p. 37.
18. *Ecstatic Confessions*, p. 95.
19. *Periphyseon*, p. 308.
20. *Periphyseon*, p. 700.
21. *Who is Man?*, p. 77.
22. *Ecstatic Confessions*, p. 37.
23. R. Ferguson (ed.), *Daily Readings with George MacLeod* (Fount, 1991), p. 21.
24. *Ecstatic Confessions*, p. 8.
25. *Ecstatic Confessions*, p. 38.
26. E. Muir, 'The Cloud', in *Collected Poems* (Faber, 1984), p. 245.
27. E. Muir, *An Autobiography* (Hogarth, 1980), pp. 48–49.
28. *An Autobiography*, p. 54.
29. A. Finkel, *In My Flesh I See God* (Aronson, 1995), p. 256.
30. Job 33:15–16.
31. Matthew 2.

Notes

32. *Periphyseon*, p. 692.
33. John 1:14.
34. Colossians 1:15.
35. Colossians 3:3.
36. Mark 2:27–28.
37. See Matthew 27.
38. Revelation 10:1; 14:14; 12:1.
39. Psalm 8:5.
40. Revelation 9:7f.
41. Revelation 12:3.
42. 'Jerusalem', in *The Complete Poetry and Prose of William Blake*, p. 177.
43. Matthew 17.
44. Hans Urs von Balthasar, 'The Unknown God', in *The von Balthasar Reader* (Crossroad, 1982), p. 186.
45. 1 John 4:16.
46. *Ecstatic Confessions*, p. 16.
47. Ephesians 3:19.

2 The Wisdom of the Self

1. Isaiah 48:4.
2. Ecclesiasticus 1:14.
3. Romans 2:15.
4. Muir, in *Collected Poems*, p. 239.
5. *Ecstatic Confessions*, p. 37.
6. *An Autobiography*, pp. 66–67.
7. Genesis 3:1f.
8. M. Buber, *Images of Good and Evil* (Routledge, 1952), p. 21.
9. Genesis 6:5.
10. *The Complete Poetry and Prose of William Blake*, p. 47.
11. 'The Four Zoas' and 'Jerusalem', in *The Complete Poetry and Prose of William Blake*, pp. 406, 198.
12. *Who is Man?*, p. 6.
13. 'Jerusalem', in *The Complete Poetry and Prose of William Blake*, pp. 179, 248.
14. *An Autobiography*, p. 145.
15. *An Autobiography*, p. 150.

Notes

16. Matthew 18:3.
17. Ecclesiasticus 1:14.
18. *Who is Man?*, p. 88.
19. Proverbs 8:30f.
20. *An Autobiography*, pp. 160–61.
21. Matthew 7:13.
22. *Abraham Isaac Kook*, p. 315.
23. Isaiah 48:6.
24. *Ecstatic Confessions*, p. 21.
25. *The Complete Poetry and Prose of William Blake*, p. 656.
26. *The Essential Kabbalah*, p. 1.
27. Matthew 13:52.
28. Ecclesiasticus 10:22.
29. *Abraham Isaac Kook*, p. 167.
30. 'Jerusalem', in *The Complete Poetry and Prose of William Blake*, p. 156.
31. *An Autobiography*, pp. 163–64.
32. *The Essential Kabbalah*, p. 108.
33. *Abraham Isaac Kook*, p. 216.
34. Luke 11:52.
35. Luke 10:36.
36. Matthew 13:34.
37. Luke 12:57.
38. Luke 17:21.
39. Isaiah 30:21.
40. *Ecstatic Confessions*, p. 36.
41. John 7:15.
42. Matthew 7:28f.
43. Matthew 5:21f.
44. A. Nolan, *Jesus Before Christianity* (DLT, 1998), p. 151.
45. Matthew 9:8.
46. Isaiah 45:3.
47. 1 Corinthians 2:7.
48. *The Essential Kabbalah*, p. 124.
49. *Who is Man?*, p. 45.
50. Wisdom 16:14,28.
51. Mark 1:35; Luke 6:12.
52. Luke 2:19; 10:39.
53. Proverbs 8:22f.

54. Wisdom 6:14.
55. Proverbs 8:4,35f.
56. Proverbs 9:10f.
57. Isaiah 42:9.
58. Wisdom 6:24.
59. Wisdom 16:14.
60. John 8:32.
61. John 18:37.
62. Isaiah 11:2.
63. 1 Corinthians 1:24.
64. 1 Corinthians 2:6.
65. 1 Corinthians 1:25.
66. Matthew 11:25.
67. 1 Corinthians 2:10f.
68. Colossians 2:3.
69. *An Autobiography*, p. 246.
70. 'Jerusalem', in *The Complete Poetry and Prose of William Blake*, p. 171.
71 Proverbs 8:20,31.
72 Luke 10:27f.
73 Isaiah 42:7.

3 *The Strength of the Self*

1. Ecclesiasticus 17:3.
2. Isaiah 52:1.
3. Psalm 77:15.
4. Psalm 46:9.
5. Ezekiel 1:24.
6. Luke 1:51–52.
7. Isaiah 49:15.
8. Isaiah 45:4–5.
9. Luke 17:21.
10. Psalm 45:6.
11. Psalm 65:6; 102:25.
12. Isaiah 27:1.
13. Psalm 68:5.
14. Ezekiel 30:20f.

Notes

15. Matthew 27:24.
16. Revelation 9:2.
17. Luke 8:30.
18. Luke 9:1.
19. Amos 5:21,24.
20. Hosea 13:8.
21. Ephesians 4:26.
22. Luke 10:27.
23. John 2:15.
24. Luke 4:18.
25. *An Autobiography*, p. 28.
26. *An Autobiography*, p. 23.
27. 'The Horses', in *Collected Poems*, pp. 246–47.
28. Matthew 17:20.
29. Matthew 9:22; Luke 7:50.
30. Psalm 136.
31. Isaiah 46:4.
32. Jeremiah 31:3; Isaiah 44:21.
33. Psalm 103:10.
34. Isaiah 55:7.
35. Wisdom 11:24.
36. *The Essential Kabbalah*, p. 87.
37. Genesis 9:2.
38. Matthew 5:43–44.
39. Luke 6:32.
40. Matthew 5:44–45.
41. John 15:12.
42. Matthew 19:19.
43. *Ecstatic Confessions*, pp. 18–19.
44. *Periphyseon*, p. 200.
45. 'Jerusalem', in *The Complete Poetry and Prose of William Blake*, p. 146.
46. John 13:34.
47. Galatians 5:13.
48. Matthew 16:24.
49. Matthew 20:25–26.
50. Genesis 11:4.
51. Matthew 4:8–10.
52. Ezekiel 34.

53. Isaiah 1:15.
54. B.R. Rees (ed.), *The Letters of Pelagius and His Followers* (Boydell, 1991), p. 76.
55. Matthew 25:42-43.
56. Matthew 5:17.
57. Matthew 23:23-24.
58. Galatians 5:1.
59. 'The Garden of Love', in *The Complete Poetry and Prose of William Blake*, p. 26.
60. Psalm 105:4.
61. Isaiah 40:31.
62. 1 Corinthians 1:24.
63. Isaiah 53:1.
64. Isaiah 53:12.
65. John 15:13.
66. Matthew 16:22-23.
67. Luke 22.
68. Luke 24:39.
69. 'Jerusalem', in *The Complete Poetry and Prose of William Blake*, p. 256.
70. 'Jerusalem', in *The Complete Poetry and Prose of William Blake*, p. 258.
71. Luke 23:34.
72. Luke 23:46.
73. Deuteronomy 33:27.
74. Isaiah 41:10.

4 The Beauty of the Self

1. Isaiah 33:17.
2. G. MacDonald, 'The Day Boy and The Night Girl', in *Fairy Tales* (Fifield, 1906), pp. 363f.
3. 'One Foot in Eden', in *Collected Poems*, p. 227.
4. Ezekiel 28:12.
5. W. Dosick, *Soul Judaism* (Jewish Lights Publishing, 1999), p. 65.
6. Song of Songs 4:1,7.
7. Matthew 13:44.

Notes

8. 'One Foot in Eden', in *Collected Poems*, p. 227.
9. 3 Maccabees 1:9.
10. 1 Kings 9:3.
11. 1 Corinthians 3:16.
12. 1 Peter 3:4.
13. Hebrews 9:11.
14. 'Jerusalem', in *The Complete Poetry and Prose of William Blake*, p. 203.
15. Luke 17:20.
16. *Ecstatic Confessions*, p. 95.
17. *Ecstatic Confessions*, p. 38.
18. 'The Brothers', in *Collected Poems*, p. 272.
19. Isaiah 3:24.
20. *An Autobiography*, pp. 91–92.
21. *An Autobiography*, p. 275.
22. Isaiah 27:1.
23. Revelation 12:9.
24. 'Jerusalem', in *The Complete Poetry and Prose of William Blake*, p. 179.
25. Psalm 74:4.
26. 1 Maccabees 2:12.
27. 'Jerusalem', in *The Complete Poetry and Prose of William Blake*, pp. 146–47.
28. B. Griffiths, *Return to the Centre* (Fount, 1976).
29. J. P. Newell, *Listening for the Heartbeat of God* (SPCK, 1997).
30. Isaiah 43:4.
31. Genesis 9:16.
32. Ezekiel 36:33f.
33. *An Autobiography*, p. 64.
34. *An Autobiography*, p. 193.
35. 'The Everlasting Gospel', in *The Complete Poetry and Prose of William Blake*, p. 520.
36. *Ecstatic Confessions*, p. 39.
37. Ezekiel 43:11.
38. *Periphyseon*, p. 184.
39. John 8:32.
40. John 1:18.
41. John 2:13f.
42. *The Letters of Pelagius*, p. 62.

Notes

43. Matthew 15:10f.
44. Matthew 23:25–26.
45. 'Jerusalem', in *The Complete Poetry and Prose of William Blake*, p. 152.
46. Hebrews 4:12.
47. 'Jerusalem', in *The Complete Poetry and Prose of William Blake*, p. 194.
48. *Ecstatic Confessions*, p. 22.
49. *Periphyseon*, p. 574.
50. Wisdom 13:3.
51. Ezekiel 16:25.
52. Isaiah 52:15.
53. Isaiah 53:2–3.
54. Judges 19:25.
55. 2 Samuel 11.
56. Isaiah 51:3.
57. Isaiah 58:10.
58. Luke 4:18.
59. Psalm 85:10.
60. Psalm 24:7; 84:10.
61. Luke 17:20.

5 The Creativity of the Self

1. My own treatment of this subject reflects the limitations of my maleness. For a more complete treatment we need the experience and the perspectives of both men and women. For a good example of this, see James Nelson and Sandra Longfellow (eds.), *Sexuality and the Sacred* (Mowbray, 1994).
2. Ezekiel 1:26.
3. Ezekiel 8:2.
4. John 1:9.
5. Job 38:29.
6. Genesis 5:3.
7. Genesis 1:26.
8. *Periphyseon*, p. 160.
9. Ecclesiasticus 43:27.
10. Romans 11:36.

Notes

11. Wisdom 12:1.
12. *The Essential Kabbalah*, pp. 59–60.
13. *The Essential Kabbalah*, p. 90.
14. Luke 3:16.
15. O. Davies (ed.), *Hildegaard of Bingen: Mystical Writings* (Crossroad, 1990), pp. 91f.
16. 'Letters', in *The Complete Poetry and Prose of William Blake*, p. 712.
17. Genesis 17:11.
18. Deuteronomy 32:18.
19. 'The Journey Back', in *Collected Poems*, p. 168.
20. *An Autobiography*, p. 236.
21. *An Autobiography*, p. 281.
22. 'Embracing Masculinity', in *Sexuality and the Sacred*, pp. 195f.
23. 'Jerusalem', in *The Complete Poetry and Prose of William Blake*, p. 198.
24. 'Jerusalem', in *The Complete Poetry and Prose of William Blake*, p. 251.
25. 'Jerusalem', in *The Complete Poetry and Prose of William Blake*, p. 205.
26. M. Eliade, *Images and Symbols* (Sheed & Ward, 1969), p. 9.
27. 'Jerusalem', in *The Complete Poetry and Prose of William Blake*, p. 158.
28. Genesis 1:28.
29. *Essential Kabbalah*, p. 157.
30. *Essential Kabbalah*, p. 155.
31. Isaiah 11:5.
32. Proverbs 8:25f.
33. Song of Songs 5:1.
34. Song of Songs 4:16.
35. Song of Songs 2:3.
36. Song of Songs 5:4–6.
37. *Periphyseon*, p. 654.
38. W. Gardner (ed.), 'Spring', in *Poems and Prose of Gerard Manley Hopkins* (Penguin, 1953), p. 28.
39. Wisdom 7:2.
40. Ecclesiasticus 7:27.
41. Song of Songs 2:7.
42. Genesis 1:31.

Notes

43. *The Essential Kabbalah*, p. 99.
44. Genesis 2:25.
45. Genesis 3:7.
46. Genesis 19.
47. Wisdom 17:14.
48. Ezekiel 37:1f.
49. Ezekiel 47:12.
50. Genesis 1:2.
51. Revelation 21:5.
52. Isaiah 46:4.
53. John 7:38.
54. Revelation 22:17.
55. Isaiah 43:19.

6 The Eternity of the Self

1. 1 Corinthians 3:6.
2. 2 Chronicles 3:15–17.
3. Ecclesiasticus 42:17.
4. Psalm 90:2.
5. Psalm 24:7.
6. Genesis 32.
7. Hebrews 9:11.
8. P. Epstein, *Kabbalah: the Way of the Jewish Mystic* (Shambhala, 1988), p. 45.
9. *Ecstatic Confessions*, p. 3.
10. 'Jerusalem', in *The Complete Poetry and Prose of William Blake*, p. 180.
11. 'Jerusalem', in *The Complete Poetry and Prose of William Blake*, p. 158.
12. 'The Four Zoas', in *The Complete Poetry and Prose of William Blake*, p. 406.
13. 'Jerusalem', in *The Complete Poetry and Prose of William Blake*, p. 225.
14. 'The Marriage of Heaven and Hell', in *The Complete Poetry and Prose of William Blake*, p. 36.
15. 'Auguries of Innocence', in *The Complete Poetry and Prose of William Blake*, p. 490.

Notes

16. Isaiah 6:3.
17. Ezekiel 10:4.
18. Ezekiel 43:2.
19. Ecclesiasticus 42:22.
20. 1 Corinthians 15:41.
21. K. White, 'The House of Insight', in *The Bird Path* (Mainstream, 1989), p. 145.
22. *The Essential Kabbalah*, p. 50.
23. R. Ferguson (ed.), *The Whole Earth Shall Cry Glory* (Wild Goose, 1985), p. 11.
24. A. Carmichael, *Carmina Gadelica* (Floris, 1994), p. 43.
25. *Carmina Gadelica*, p. 286.
26. *Ecstatic Confessions*, p. 149.
27. Genesis 28:16–17.
28. Luke 9:33.
29. 1 Kings 8:27.
30. *The Essential Kabbalah*, p. 63.
31. 'God's Grandeur', in *Poems and Prose of Gerard Manley Hopkins*, p. 27.
32. 'The House of Insight' and 'The Cold Wind of Dawn', in *The Bird Path*, pp. 142, 31.
33. 'Jerusalem', in *The Complete Poetry and Prose of William Blake*, p. 157.
34. 'Jerusalem', in *The Complete Poetry and Prose of William Blake*, p. 225.
35. Isaiah 37:31.
36. *The Essential Kabbalah*, p. 70.
37. 'God's Grandeur', in *Poems and Prose of Gerard Manley Hopkins*, p. 27.
38. 'The Marriage of Heaven and Hell', in *The Complete Poetry and Prose of William Blake*, p. 39.
39. 'The Transfiguration', in *Collected Poems*, pp. 198f.
40. *An Autobiography*, pp. 192–93.
41. John 1:51.
42. John 1:14.
43. Colossians 2:9.
44. 1 Corinthians 2:8.
45. John 19:33.
46. Colossians 3:3.

Notes

47. Romans 8:21.
48. Wisdom 2:23.
49. G. MacDonald, *Lilith* (Eerdmans, 1981), p. 147.
50. 'The Marriage of Heaven and Hell', in *The Complete Poetry and Prose of William Blake*, p. 39.
51. Matthew 16:25.
52. 'That Nature is a Heraclitean Fire', in *Poems and Prose of Gerard Manley Hopkins*, pp. 65–66.
53. 'As kingfishers catch fire', in *Poems and Prose of Gerard Manley Hopkins*, p. 51.
54. 1 Corinthians 3:10f.
55. M. Williamson, *Return to Love* (Harper Collins, 1992), p. 165.
56. 'The Transfiguration', in *Collected Poems*, p. 198f.
57. Isaiah 45:8.
58. *In My Flesh I See God*, p. 279.

7 The Presence of the Self

1. Ezekiel 43:7.
2. Hebrew 9:11.
3. Isaiah 54:5.
4. Matthew 1:23; Isaiah 6:14.
5. John 10:30.
6. Matthew 28:9.
7. A. Bond (ed.), *Body* (Bookman Schwartz, 1997), p. 157.
8. John 12:3.
9. Luke 7:36f.
10. John 12:6.
11. Amos 5:24.
12. Psalm 96:13.
13. Psalm 98:9.
14. Isaiah 52:7.
15. Luke 1:52.
16. 1 Corinthians 12:12.
17. Isaiah 54:10.
18. Song of Songs 8:6.
19. Song of Songs 2:14.
20. Isaiah 62:4.

Notes

21. R. S. Pine-Coffin (ed.), *Saint Augustine Confessions* (Penguin, 1961), p. 231.
22. Isaiah 50:2.
23. Isaiah 65:1.
24. Isaiah 44:22.
25. 'Jerusalem', in *The Complete Poetry and Prose of William Blake*, p. 199.
26. Luke 6:4.
27. Matthew 27:51.
28. John 1:10.
29. Ezekiel 1:15f.
30. Luke 10:41f.
31. Genesis 2:2.
32. Exodus 20:8.
33. Exodus 3:5.
34. Luke 18:16.
35. *Who is Man?*, p. 116.
36. Matthew 28:20.
37. *Kabbalah: the Way of the Jewish Mystic*, p. 157.
38. Matthew 6:34.
39. Psalm 69:1–2.
40. John 13.
41. Matthew 18:22.
42. *An Autobiography*, p. 270.
43. Luke 15:11f.
44. *Who is Man?*, p. 45.
45. As quoted by E. Johnson, *She Who Is*, p. 228.
46. 1 John 4:16.
47. *Who is Man?*, p. 46.
48. Song of Songs 2:10.
49. Song of Songs 5:3.
50. Song of Songs 5:6.
51. Song of Songs 7:11–12.
52. *In My Flesh I See God*, p. 247.
53. 'Jerusalem', in *The Complete Poetry and Prose of William Blake*, p. 152.
54. Psalm 36:8.
55. *I and Thou*, p. 82.
56. Psalm 42:1.

57. Matthew 9:9.
58. 'The Return', in *Collected Poems*, p. 166.
59. Psalm 105:4.